Wh   Enterprise
re

Exploring the context of an enterprise

Tom Graves

Published by
JC3DVIS

www.jc3dvis.co.uk

First published November 2023
ISBN 9781739125455 (Paperback)
First Edition

Legal disclaimer

This book is presented solely for educational purposes. The
authors and publisher are not offering it as legal, accounting,
or other professional services advice. While best efforts have
been used in preparing this book, the authors and publisher
make no representations or warranties of any kind and
assume no liabilities of any kind with respect to the accuracy
or completeness of the contents and specifically disclaim any
implied warranties of merchantability or fitness of use for
a particular purpose. Neither the authors nor the publisher
shall be held liable or responsible to any person or entity with
respect to any loss or incidental or consequential damages
caused, or alleged to have been caused, directly or indirectly,
by the information contained herein.

CGI illustrations, design and editing by JC3DVIS

Whole Enterprise Architecture

Architecture

Exploring the context of an enterprise

Tom Graves

Contents

Part 3: Why Whole EA?

Part 4: Whole EA perspectives

Part 5: How not to fail in EA

Part 6: Appendix

What is *Whole Enterprise Architecture?*

To some, enterprise architecture is a bit of a mystery. *"Something to do with IT and enterprises?"* It can seem full of jargon and complex diagrams. But at its heart is about making things better and working *'on purpose'*. It is about connecting the dots and understanding the big picture.

In this book an **enterprise** is defined as:
A bold endeavour, an undertaking. For example, running an airport might be described as one type of enterprise, while the passengers' enterprise would be to get to their holiday as quickly and safely as possible.

And **architecture** is defined as:
The structure and story of how everything works together as a whole. In an airport for example, a building architect would tackle the physical aspects of the building, the air-conditioning, doors etc. A solution architect would tackle the IT aspects of the airport, such as the software needed to run the airport, assisting: visas, luggage, information flow, people flow, governance and much more, while an enterprise architect would tackle all of the parts of an enterprise, connecting the boxes.

So **Whole enterprise architecture** is defined as:
Understanding the overall story of the enterprise about everything in the enterprise, not just one aspect such as IT. Understanding the connections, the *'whys'*. Being able to see the big-picture, understanding the mess and unnecessary duplication. It's about the context of the enterprise.

Throughout this book we will use an example of an airport to demonstrate various concepts, as it is a vastly complex enterprise, yet familiar enough to most people.

This book acts as a bridge to a huge library of work produced over thirty years in the field of enterprise architecture.
Most of the chapters reference more *'in-depth'* articles which can be found in a set of anthologies *at www.leanpub.com/u/tetradian* .

Tom Graves has been an independent consultant for more than four decades, in business transformation, enterprise architecture and knowledge management. His clients in Europe, Australasia and the Americas cover a broad range of industries including small-business, banking, utilities,manufacturing, logistics, engineering, media, telecoms, research, defence and government. He has a special interest in whole-enterprise architectures for non-profit, social, government and commercial enterprises.

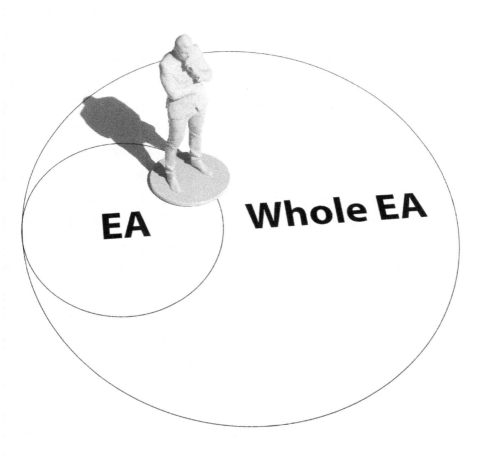

EA

Whole EA

Part 1:

Enterprise Architecture as a career

This section of the book is an abridged version of
'Creating a career in Enterprise Architecture'
www.leanpub.com/tp-career

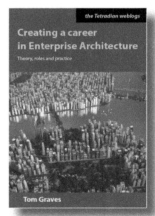

1: Creating a career in EA

What is Enterprise-Architecture?

IT-architecture is a cross-disciplinary specialism: the enterprise IT architect will bridge between the various IT specialties, but the focus essentially remains centred around IT alone. By contrast, to the enterprise-architect, everywhere and nowhere is *'the centre'*: they must be a generalist, interested in everything. So I would encourage you to lift your eyes from the screen and the imaginary worlds within IT-systems, and look around you. IT systems describe a digital world, but they are also very physical: they exist in a real world beyond data alone. A real, messy, chaotic world, where computers need power and to be kept cool, placed somewhere safe from dust, rain and more. And a human world, where real people have real emotions and do the real work, and where passion for code *(and, sometimes, a confused passion for 'control')* is what creates all of this in the first place.

Within enterprise-architecture itself, look wider than just IT-oriented frameworks[1], to models[2] that encompass more of the *overall* enterprise. I would suggest to keep remembering that enterprise architecture literally means *'the architecture of the enterprise'*, not merely the architecture of the enterprise-IT. The IT exists within the context and needs of the broader organisation; and the organisation exists within the context and needs of a far broader shared-enterprise. An organisation is bounded by rules, roles and responsibilities, but an enterprise is essentially a human construction, bounded by aspirations, commitments, hopes, and fears. We create an enterprise-architecture *for* an organisation, but *about* that broader enterprise. And *'quality'* in all its forms is what arises from that broader enterprise: creating all those quality-oriented issues in architecture such as reliability, efficiency, safety, sustainability, security and more. If you remember to keep that idea of the broader enterprise in mind whilst you work on even the smallest item of code, it will help to show you what an *'enterprise'* really is, and so the nature of enterprise-architecture itself. The last point, perhaps, is to respect that all of this does take time, many years. But you're already a long way down that track: say, after more than ten years in *'the trade'* you will certainly have learned a great deal about the difference between academic theory and real-world practice!

---

1. Framework

A EA framework is a collection of methods, best practices, and tools to tackle a specific type of problem, often affected by change. An early example is DODAF, which in basic terms is a checklist of recommended items to explore and how to tackle them, such as unwanted duplication of equipment.

2. Models

For example in an airport, where experts model how the people flow through the airport, what order to do they do things, what depends on what and how they interact. In this example we are modelling the customer journey.

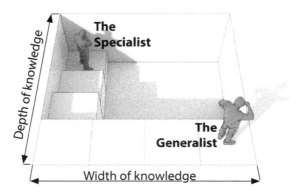

The Specialist versus the Generalist

Are you a specialist or generalist?

The relationship between specialist and generalist is rarely an easy one…
but if you want to be involved in EA, then it's a relationship that you're going
to need to resolve. And, perhaps most of all, resolve it within yourself…

Long ago, it was not all that unusual for an individual to become a *'complete
generalist'*: someone with deep skill in everything, or at least, everything that
was known at the time.
But these days, no-one could do this: the vast scope of information,
knowledge and skills that could apply in our world means that any one
person would need many lifetimes to learn them all. And yet we have to able
to get things done right here, right now.

Think of this as two axes: horizontal, for width of knowledge, and vertical, for
depth of knowledge. The usual solution is to specialise, and then perhaps to
over-specialise. The danger of over-specialism, though, is that we risk losing
the ability to *'connect the dots'*: we get better and better at *'doing things
right'*, but we lose the ability to know if we're *'doing the right things'*. So we
need some means to link all those specialists together: and that's where the
generalist comes into the picture. ***Enterprise-architects are specialists at
being generalists.***

***In most current cultures, specialism is still prized far more than
generalism***. One of the reasons is that specialists visibly *do* things, whereas
generalists don't seem to *do* much at all. It is the connections *between* things
which are difficult to describe or to value.

To quote the *Tao Te Ching*:

*"…therefore profit comes from what is there;
usefulness from what is not there."*

No matter how useful the generalism of enterprise-architecture may be, the visible *'profit'* will usually *seems* to come only from the specialists. It is really important to recognise that **specialist generalists are depth-specialists, they specialise in the skills required for broadscope generalism**. The focus is not so much on content, as a discipline-specialist would, but on how different disciplines link together.

Some of the skills-challenges here include:
• thinking in multiple domain[1] *'languages'* at the same time, and translating between them as required
• thinking and designing in terms of interdependent systems rather than single independent specialities
• thinking in and working with multiple time-perspectives, in some cases ranging from sub-microseconds to millennia
• identifying, and rapidly learning, the key principles and practices of new domains, and requirements for and implications of linking between them
• clarifying and communicating contexts, constraints, designs and design-issues
• searching for simplicity
• mastering the *'soft-skills[2]'* needed for negotiation and suchlike, in what will always be a challenging and highly *'political'* area of work

One challenge will be around learning all those many different domains: *'just enough detail'* to be useful, yet no more than that, because you simply won't have time to do any more than that.
For every discipline that your work will touch, you'll need to learn enough about it not only to be able to converse credibly with any of the specialists in that area, but do so in ways that will enable you to make connections between all of those domains, connections that the specialists probably won't even know could exist. There are some personal challenges, too: such as the embarrassment of having to admit to others that *"I don't know"*, for example.

---

1. Domain
For some the meaning of the word 'domain' might be obvious, but for others maybe not. A domain might be described as an area of knowledge. For example an airport security expert's domain would be 'security'.
So domain language might be specific terms or shorthand, such as in cyber-security: 'Incident handling'.

2. Soft skills
Skills which are needed for all professions, such as teamwork, while 'Hard skills' are only required for certain industries.

Where do we start with EA?

You're an experienced enterprise-architect, having spent most your working life in one industry. You now have a new job, in a new company, in an industry that's entirely new to you. And the company at present has no architecture at all: you're 'it'. Where on earth do you start?

In essence, we start from scratch.

Which means that several threads need to start straight away, somewhat in parallel:
• the politics and pragmatics[1] of architecture
• setting the stage, the *'big-picture'*
• finding allies, people who know *'the trade'*
• establishing standards
• finding the story

The first point is that everything about any form of enterprise architecture is intensely *'political'*, in several different senses, which means we need to face the politics of this straight away. Probably the single most important concern is to get *'buy-in'* at senior level, certainly from the respective Chief executive officer for the main focus area *(e.g. the Chief information officer, for enterprise IT-architecture)*, but preferably from the CEO and entire executive. If you don't have that *'buy-in'*, you'll be going nowhere: you need to get the executive on-side.

As others state, the key to getting the executive on-side, and everyone else on-side, too, is communication. One valuable aspect of this is to get them personally engaged in describing the big-picture of the overall context in which the organisation operates, and where the organisation fits within that context. In effect, what we would do here is identify the high-level *'why'* for which the organisation is a *'how'*, in other words, the *'why'* that provides the anchor for all of the organisation's strategy. I usually look through sources such as the organisation's website, publications, advertisements, intranet and annual-reports. There's usually enough information there to build some preliminary models with which started: or at least, enough for people to tell us that the models are wrong, which is one way of getting them engaged in telling us their ideas about what it should be!

---

1. Pragmatics
Linguistics uses this complex term to broadly describe different methods of communication, including non-verbal communication.
For example a meeting can suddenly change its whole mood, depending on how one person might talk to another.

While we're doing this, we need to be looking for any allies, people who are already committed to other themes that connect with EA, and would be likely to see the value of connecting between those areas of interest. This is really important if we've only just started with the organisation, because enterprise-architectures depend greatly on person-to-person conversations and connections: knowing who to talk with, and how to talk with them, will depend in turn on backgrounds and credibility and personal-networks within that organisation that often take five or more years to develop.

Those are people we need as allies: and finding them is one of our first and most urgent priorities as soon as we start work at new place. Despite all those models and the rest, what really drives the architecture, what makes it happen, in real-world practice, is person-to-person conversations.

Another concern that those allies can help us with straight away is in identifying the standards that apply in the context. Some standards would apply to just about every industry. Other standards will be generic for the industry as a whole, but they're usually not hard to find.

What we are also looking for are all the other standards, guidelines and workarounds that are specific to this organisation, some of which, perhaps many, may not exist anywhere in any written form. And that again is where our allies can be really helpful, because otherwise we would have little chance to know what these are.

We also need to be on the lookout for standards that should be there, and aren't. Which can be a little bit tricky, from a political perspective, not least because it tends to highlight issues that people *'should'* have known about already, and didn't… Once again, our allies will be invaluable here, in finding ways to introduce these ideas, and to smooth out any ruffled-feathers that may arise.

One trap to watch for is to beware of bringing too many assumptions from our previous organisation and industry: many of those assumptions will not work in this new context. The skills and experience of *'how to do architecture'* are probably the only part of the work that will remain unchanged: we need to be able and willing to challenge ourselves on just about everything other than that.

Almost all of that above is about enterprise-architecture as structure. The other side is about about architecture as story. This is enormously important: story is emotive; story embeds meaning; story engages. Stories matter: in a very real sense, everything about the architecture is or represents or describes a story. Even the enterprise itself is a story. Which means that it's well worth while to go *'looking for the story'*.

I typically look for all of those interweaving stories that hold everything together. Some of these stories are straightforward enough: every journey through a business-process is a story; every customer-experience or *'value-journey'[1]* holds a story; every transaction is part of a story that extends far beyond the transaction itself.

Yet there are also the many stories that employees and others tell themselves, and tell each other, about what works, about what doesn't. About what is or is not valued in practice within the organisation. About workarounds or special-cases that no-one has documented but without which the store or office would not work.
Those stories are often really important from a structure-perspective[2], too. And there's the story, or stories, that the organisation tells about itself, about how it positions itself in the market, about what it values most and would most like to share with others; and the stories that others in turn tell about the organisation, including whether they believe that the organisation holds to its purported values. Those last stories are some of the most essential real-world feedback for strategy, which in turn feeds back into changes in structure, in the *what, how, where* and *when* of the conventional EA.

The need for a quick-start is very real. We need quick results, but above all we need to get the interest and, if possible, real excitement, going right from day one. We have to make sure that EA matters to everyone, in their context, their workspace, because without that engagement and excitement, this will go nowhere.

Do not try to start off straight away with any of the *'heavyweight'* frameworks[4]. They do have very real value, in later stages of EA *(though often only in specific areas of EA)*. For this earliest stage, we need something simpler.

---

1. Value-journey
With an airport example, from the customer's perspective the whole airport is only a small part of their value-journey. For them they want to spend as little time as possible in the airport, as their destination is what is important to them.

2. Structure[3]-perspective
In the structure of an airport, if someone wanted to improve security checks, exploring all the elements such as x-ray scanners and software currently used. From this one could begin to work out what might need upgrading, for example.

3. The 'structure' of the architecture of the enterprise.
In an airport example, the structure might be made of parts, such as security, which works in a certain way and slots together with other parts in the airport.

4. Heavyweight framework
A framework which tries to give every type of detail, but it won't work in every context, while lightweight frameworks are often a set of check-lists.

I usually describe EA, development in terms of six distinct steps:

Step 0: Get started. *(the initial setup to do EA)*
Step 1: Establishing what business are we in. *(The big-picture)*
Step 2: Clean up. *(horizontal optimisation[1])*
Step 3: From strategy and execution. *(top-down[2])*
Step 4: The plan versus the real world. *(bottom-up[3])*
Step 5: Resolving pain-points[4]. *(spiral-outwards[5])*

'Heavyweight' frameworks tend to come into their own in **Step 2** and
Step 3. But before that happens, we need to have done the **Step 1** work
of establishing the enterprise-context, and before that, we need to have
established, in **Step 0**, the reason and desire for doing EA at all.

Better frameworks emphasise that the very first step after someone in the
organisation decides to do something about EA, is a first-stage
training, education, above all communication.

Getting to know the background is also crucial, though most of it will
happen after that first *'Step-0 stage'*. These must include concerns such as
identifying vision, values and mission. Also being clear about the crucial
difference between *'the organisation' and 'the enterprise'*, because they're
not the same.
Another really important point here: don't fall into the trap of describing
enterprise IT-architecture (EITA) as 'enterprise-architecture' (EA).

---

1. Horizontal optimisation
*In an airport, making sure each part of the airport works as efficiently as
possible, for example reducing duplication in security.*

2. Top-down
Decisions made by the heads of an organisation which filter down to all staff.

3. Bottom-up
*Staff communicating with higher ranking staff if the plans are actually working
in the real world.*

4. Pain-points
*An airport example might be, where people are trying to get through border
control, but the security system goes down.*

5. Spiral outwards
*In an airport, rather than picking a top-down view, we could pick anywhere,
such as baggage claim and looking up, down, sideways to see how any point in
the airport connects to everything else.*

Everything up to this point has been, and must be, about *real whole-enterprise architecture*, because we must establish the overall scope before we can focus in on any specific part such as *EITA*, security, business-architecture or anything else.

If we constrain the scope too early, we're then left with no adequate means to connect to the other area architectures, which again would guarantee architectural failure, especially over the longer term.

This, by the way, is another reason why we don't try to use 'heavyweight' frameworks for EA until such time as we do want to focus specifically on the IT related areas.

The other theme, around principles and standards, is something that we should not worry about too much until we've already gone some way down the track. At that point the only thing we need to say about principles and standards is that we are indeed going to need principles and standards, and how to apply those principles and standards to real-world practice. That's it.

Any competent architect will know that yes, we will definitely need security and governance principles. But in the early stages all you need to do is add them to a list of examples. It doesn't need anything more that that, for that stage. Later on, yes, you'll need a lot more detail. But we don't try to do that too early: all it would do is confuse people, drowning them in too-much-detail and putting them off, just at the point when we need to gain their engagement.

So, quick summary: find a way to live with the frustration, because it's going to be there for a quite a while, whatever you do; and do settle down to do everything step-by-step, because it is the only way that works.

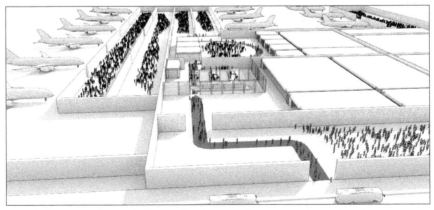

Simple frameworks can help you begin to evaluate complex enterprises, such as how an airport could function more effectively.

⬠⬠⬠⬠⬠ *Taken from the chapter: **Creating a career in enterprise-architecture***

2: The unique contribution of EA

What do enterprise-architects actually do?

It's not that enterprise-architects should attempt to do anything to do with business: that's micro-management, not architecture. Instead, what architects do is connect: we join the dots, link between the boxes, build bridges between the silos, get people talking with each other, to help create a clear sense of the whole as whole. To be honest, architecture doesn't do much of anything that's visible on the surface: and most its deliverables don't make much sense in those terms, either. Most of the *'doing'* within an enterprise is the role and purview of area-specialists, whereas architects are cross-functional generalists whose real role is is to connect between things. *Architecture connects*: that's its real purpose.

An architecture needs to be able to connect between anything and everything that's in scope for the context of that architecture. It doesn't attempt to do everything that's in scope: but it does need to understand everything that's in scope, in *just enough detail*, and with awareness of what and how *it depends* on what, in order to unify and connect between everything and everything else that's in scope for the context of that architecture.

If something is in scope for an architecture, it's *'in scope'* because something else depends on it being there: so if the architecture can't connect between everything that's in scope, the architecture as a whole could be placed at risk. To be viable, an architecture must be able to connect everything in scope with everything else in scope. It's the connections that are the real focus of interest for the enterprise-architecture, not necessarily the *'somethings'* themselves.

In reality, everything depends in some way, either directly or indirectly, upon everything else: so the only way that works is to recognise that everywhere and nowhere is *'the centre of the architecture'*, all at the same time. As soon as we make out that some one area is *'the centre'* of the architecture by definition we'll have broken the unity and symmetry of the architecture, which means we'd have also set it up for failure in some *'unexpected'* way.

The unique contribution of architecture is that it connects, helps make whole, helps link strategy to execution, intent to action, action to value, and so on. Enterprise-architecture is just another expression of the same idea: architecture at an enterprise scope, architecture whose scope is *'the enterprise'*. Yet specialists will only work within their own specific areas, often without much if any sense of connection with anything else: so the unique contribution of EA is that it can connect everything and anything across all of the enterprise, to create that whole as unified-whole.

⬠⬠⬠⬠⬠ *Taken from the chapter:* **The unique contribution of enterprise-architecture**

3: How much should an EA know & do?

How much should an EA aim to *'architect the enterprise'*?
Architecture itself must always face toward the *'big picture'* view; there's also always a large component of real, practical, concrete design, because architecture only becomes useful when it does touch the real world. So an architect is also always a designer, a creator of what people then experience as *'architecture'* in the real world.

But there's an interesting trade-off here. The clients must always be not merely involved, but deeply engaged in the design. If that doesn't happen, they won't feel that they own it *('own' as personal responsibility, that is, rather than mere possession)*. And if they don't feel that commitment towards it, that it is their choice, their creation, rather than something imposed on them, the structure will fail, if only because they'll find themselves fighting against it in all manner of small subtle ways, consciously or not. To make that happen, the architect needs to obtain all of those things from the clients, and so does need to be a firm yet genuinely humble facilitator.

At the same time, each architect does need to express their own choices in the architecture: every building by Gehry or Gaudi, Frank Lloyd Wright or Charles Rennie Mackintosh, is instantly recognisable as such. So the opinions and politics and world-view of each architect do also matter: which means that, especially as an external consultant, we do need to ensure that our views do align reasonably well with those of the respective clients, to ensure that the inevitable gaps can be bridged enough to make the architecture work. This is more about empathy than sympathy: we need to be able to listen, to respect the clients' knowledge and desires, to yield when appropriate; yet also able to respect our own knowledge, and to know when to stand our own ground. What we know and how we express our vision does matter, and that's precisely why the client employs us, after all.

How much industry/enterprise knowledge does the EA need?
What we call *'architecture'* is actually a complex mix of big-picture aspiration and real-world design. To put it at its simplest:

• design depends on 'area-specific' *specialist knowledge*
• architecture depends on 'link-between-areas' *generalist knowledge*

So we need both types of knowledge, which is why it takes a long time to become competent as an architect. But area-specific knowledge is relatively easy to acquire: almost all education and almost all organisational structures push towards specialisation of some form. So to balance that, the architect must be a consummate generalist. You need to be able to learn the basics of an area or a business very fast indeed, sometimes mere minutes may be all that you'll have, in which to get something both valid and usable enough to work with.

Even more, you need to be able not only to grasp the *'world'* of each specialist, and converse intelligently and usefully in their own specific terms, but also to link all of the *'areas'* together in new, more effective ways. We need very strong people-skills, to be able to engage the attention and commitment of people in domain and at every level, from the cleaners and call-centre workers right the way up to the boardroom.

The specialists often won't know how their worlds connect with others, if at all, so they won't be able to help you much in that: it's up to you to understand the whole as a whole, and make it work well for everyone. The reality is that there's a limit to how much any one person can know, which leads to two very different types of EA roles:

• the internal consultant, with in-depth knowledge of the organisation
• the external consultant, with in-depth knowledge of the world beyond the organisation, including the EA discipline itself

The internal consultants' value lies in what they know of their own specific business context; paradoxically, the external consultants' value often lies in what they *don't* know, and in the sometimes *'stupid'*-seeming questions they ask so as to discover what they need to know. External consultants can challenge an organisation's assumptions and *'givens'* with far more licence and freedom than most *'insiders'* would have; *'insiders'* know the organisation's deep culture in ways that would never be available to any *'outsider'*. Somehow we need to balance the two, the worst balance being where a closed group of outside specialists create *'the architecture'*, and then walk away, leaving the organisation with no architecture capability[1] of their own and no way to use the work that's been done.

Most of my own work is in the *'external consultant'* role, creating context and capability. I've done a certain amount of *'inside consultant'* work in my time, but mainly enough to gain deep respect for the fact that it takes years to build up the knowledge and connections enough to do real *whole-of-organisation* architecture from the inside. So for most of my clients, my real value is not that I know their business in detail, but that I can learn enough detail fast, and connect that to the whole of the extended-enterprise within which their own enterprise will operate and exist.

Two two key points:

• the relevant enterprise is always larger than the organisation in scope
• an organisation is bounded by rules, whereas an enterprise is bounded by shared commitment

Which means that whatever type of *'enterprise architecture'* we do, we need to know a lot more than just our own scope. IT infrastructure architects need to understand the applications and data that will run in their infrastructure; data-architects need to understand the business-use of that data as information and knowledge for decision-support; business-architects need to understand the broader enterprise.

Both horizontally *(partners, supply-chain, etc)* and vertically *(market, clients, prospects, anti-clients[1], etc)*. The in-depth knowledge of our own area is *(relatively)* easy to obtain; it's going outside our own scope that's a lot harder, simply because so much of it is literally *'alien'*.

As a consultant EA, I need to be able to translate the strangeness of those *'alien worlds'* into something that makes practical sense for my clients. I have to make those *'alien worlds'* seem safe for them, too. And I need to know all of it well enough not to make any serious mistakes! An internal-EA's knowledge is usually design focussed, literally into the depth of the detail; an external-EA's knowledge is necessarily far more generalist. The opposite of *'depth'*, in a sense, looking outward, making connections, drawing analogies and innovations from every other available discipline and area.

So how much knowledge, and what knowledge, do we really need?
A good specialist can describe and deliver *'best-practice'* for the industry. As an architect and a generalist, I need to understand what *'best-practice'* looks like at present. I need in-depth knowledge of the industry, or at least know how and where and from whom I can acquire it fast. But I also need to be able to describe and deliver far more than existing *'best practice'*. In fact something that will not only deliver *'even-better-practice'* now, but will continue to elicit new improvements to overall effectiveness onward into the future. To do that, I sometimes need to deliberately *'forget'* all of what I know about current *'best practice'* in the organisation and industry, because the broader enterprise often has different ideas, and better ideas.

To constrain the amount of needed *'depth-knowledge'* to a level that's achievable, we can usually set the scope-boundaries to those of the broader enterprise, again, always at least a couple of steps larger than whatever our own *'enterprise'* may be. If we're doing business-architecture for an airport, for example, we obviously need to understand our own business-drivers and internal business context. We need to understand the drivers and context of our immediate market: clients such as pasengers; other airports and other direct competitors; *'up-side'* and *'down-side'*. In other words, all the usual interweaving of the transaction-economy.
But we also need to understand what's happening beyond our immediate market. Especially where it interweaves with the attention-economy and trust/reputation-economy: hence the importance of non-clients, anti-clients. And other intersecting service-providers such as border control, fuel, medical services, and the community in general. What are some of the entirely different forms of travel that could sideline airports entirely?

---

1. Anti-clients
For an airport anti-clients can be all those who are opposed to the airport in some way. Local residents or disgruntled passengers. How they fit into the overall enterprise is shown overleaf, with the Whole EA tool.
Anti-clients are discussed further in chapter 28.

If we remain solely introspective, looking only at our own immediate world (*'the competition' and so on*), we can't complain if our *'enterprise'* is suddenly overwhelmed by a tsunami of change that could have been entirely expected, if only we'd had the sense to look out to sea…

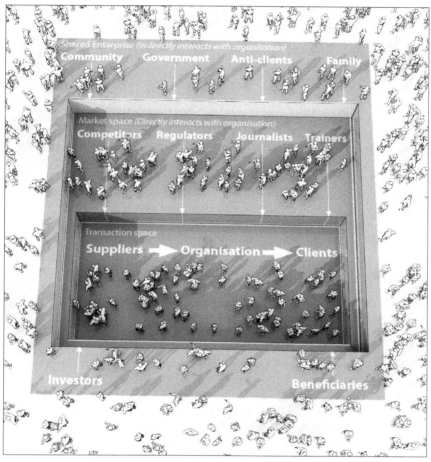

A simplified version of the Whole EA tool designed by Tom Graves and Michael Smith allows you to explore the enterprise in which an organisation sits.

⬠⬠⬠⬠⬠ *Taken from the chapter:* **How much should an enterprise-architect know and do?**

4: The deliverables of EA

Just what are the deliverables of whole-enterprise architecture?
IT-architects and process-architects would expect to deliver strategic
road-maps, application-portfolio maps and suchlike, often encompassing
their entire area; while solution-architects would be expected to deliver
detailed and fully-documented solution designs.

But whole-enterprise-architects? To any outsider, often all we seem to
do is talk...
Yet when I look at my own work, in actuality that is indeed true: my main
deliverable really is that I talk with people. I'm a generalist:
I connect things, concepts, ideas, perspectives, in often-unexpected ways,
and that really is where I deliver most of my value. I don't have much in the
way of tangible *'deliverables'*: most of the deliverables of whole-enterprise
architecture appear only in the outcomes of other people's work. Which can
be quite tricky when we have to explain our *'return on investment'* and the
like to engineers and managers, who want definite deliverables from us, to
prove that they've done their job of monitoring our job as consultants.
Here are some examples of deliverables:

• Maturity-assessment of existing methods, models and frameworks
• Assessment of EA and enterprise effectiveness
• Recommendations for EA presentation within the company
• Possible scenarios including roadmaps for further development to
  enhance models and contribute to company effectiveness and agility

The maturity-assessment and effectiveness-assessment are both developed
against documented processes, and they do both deliver a documented
score that has some definite meaning for the organisation. To a manager
or other *'outsider'*, the score is usually seen as a valid *'deliverable'* in its own
right: we've done something, and the score is the tangible result of that
item of work. Yet the reality is that the score itself is often all but irrelevant:
*the real value is in the conversation that develops around what the score
means*, in terms of what it suggests about what the organisation can do to
enhance its EA-maturity and overall effectiveness. The catch, of course, is
that to some, a conversation isn't a *'deliverable'*: it's a between-thing,
a before-things-happen-thing, and so doesn't really exist, even if though
it is actually needed in order for things to happen.

The records of the conversation itself are often of definite value: which is
why I usually take at least one camera to any consultancy session, to record
whiteboards and the like. And often also a video and/or audio-recorder as
well, to capture those fortunate yet all too-fleeting comments that didn't
make it onto the whiteboard or into anyone's notebook.

⬡⬡⬡⬡⬡ *Taken from the chapter: **The deliverables of***
enterprise-architecture

5: How I do Whole EA

Methods, Constraints, and the Individual

I describe a skill, any skill, as being made up of three components:

1. The methods used in the skill to resolve an issue, which are a combination of:
2. The real-world constraints of attempting to resolve an issue, common to all, such as language or gravity.
3. How an individual attempts to resolve an issue based on their assumptions, experience, physical ability and so on.

What I found, was that most people seem to focus on the methods used in any skill. But that actually misses the point: the methods used by any skilled person come from their own personal resolution of the constraints and they how personally attempt to resolve an issue.

This is why using someone else's methods doesn't always work, and why *'best practice'* can be dangerously misleading: the constraints of the issue remain the same, but the context is different, and so may well need different methods.

Focussing on method also makes it much more difficult to tease apart the separate threads of constraints and how an individual approaches the issue. It should be obvious that blurring the two is not likely to be a good idea, and yet that's exactly what happens whenever we focus only on method.

In all skills-work, in fact in just about every human context, we also come face to face with *Gooch's Paradox: "Things have not only to be seen to be believed, but also have to be believed to be seen"*. In an all too literal sense, in skills-work, reality is what we say it is: we actually create it, from nothing, or rather from a combination of imagination and hard work. To resolve Gooch's Paradox, we treat the *'how one person approaches the issue'* and our assumptions, **as if** they are part of the constraints of the context.

The danger is that we may forget that point about *'as if'*, and, if we think about those assumptions at all, think that they are part of the constraints of the context, rather than an random choice to resolve an issue.

Once assumptions creep in we have a context to which random constraints have been applied. Which places random limits on possibility. But the only way that we'll be able to see that the constraints are random is to step back a bit, and re-separate the individuals approach from shared constraints. Leading to *iterative 'methods to-look-at-methods'*, analysis-to-unpack-analysis, and so on. Which is what I do.

In brief I can demonstrate the *Five Element/effectiveness framework* that I use in a lot of my client-work. The first of these explores the overall context:

- **Purpose**, what are we aiming to do here? and why?
- **People**, who would be needed for this purpose?
- **Preparation**, what planning and logistics would be needed?
- **Process**, what needs to be done to achieve the purpose?
- **Performance**, what constitutes 'success', and for whom?

(A diagram showing a simplified version of the Five Elements, is shown in Chapter 6).

The other checklist is a set of keywords on **effectiveness**, which work at right angles to the Five Element set, these are:

- **Appropriate**, is this on track towards the purpose?
- **Elegant**, does this support the human-factors in the context?
- **Efficient**, does this make the best use of the available resources?
- **Reliable**, can this be relied upon to deliver the required results?
- **Integrated**, does this help to link everything to everything else?

To assess a context, we can start from anywhere at all. The point is that we use these check-lists not as linear lists, but as a reminder to keep looking round, bouncing back and forth between each of the interconnected themes in the two lists, looking at the context from every possible angle, and at every level from really-big-picture to finest-detail.

Questioning everything
Looking back at the various areas I've worked in or with, there's a fairly consistent pattern about what I've done and the sequence in which I've done it.

The first stage is just getting involved at all: taking the ideas and practices at face-value, and putting them into practice as if they are entirely *'true'*.

In my experience, there are two parts to this:

- identify the big-picture theme for the overall context
- apply design-thinking tactics to question everything

These days I tend to look for a brief overview-statement. Usually only about three to five words, that has a distinct three-part structure: it identifies the *'things'* or concerns that matter to everyone in the context, what's being done with or to those items, and why it's deemed to be important. This gives us a stable anchor to which we know we can return, and against which we can test anything in the context.

Then, following standard *'design-thinking'* tactics, we use a suite of *'disruptive'* questions about the context, for example:
• what's another version of this?
• what does this look like at a smaller scale, or a larger scale?
• what happens if we substitute something else for this?
• what happens if we invert some or all of the rules?
• is there a *'term-hijack'* here? Does a small subset appear to be the whole, blocking the view to any other part of the context?

It's very common to find aspects of the context that a) don't and can't make any sense, b) clearly don't work *'as advertised'*, and c) there are key players with a vested interest in ensuring that everything remains unquestioned and unchallenged.

A very clear, insistent emphasis on the big-picture, holding to the overall vision for the shared enterprise is essential.

We need to do this until we do start to get a clear separation between the constraints of the context and the approaches to the context, which are, by definition, individual and subjective. Then we can start to work towards new methods that work with the context under the current conditions.

Yet describing what I do, and how I do it and exactly how it delivers its very real value, can be very difficult.

There is *structure* to it, but it's not the usual kind of structure that most people seem to expect in this type of work.

There is a distinct *process* to it, but it's often not a linear step-by step process, in the usual sense. Yes, there are step-by-step elements in it, and to it, but the overall process is almost anything but linear in nature.

The *answers* we need do arise in the process. But it's not about *'answers'* as such. Indeed, often its most important attribute is that it helps people find the right questions, the ones they didn't know about, the ones that they most needed to find for themselves.

It's *partially predictable*, but only in the sense that it does lead to real outcomes, as above. The problem is that often we won't and can't know beforehand exactly what each outcome will be. In effect, it's dominated by the three-part *'Enterprise-Architects' Mantra'*, of *'I don't know'*, *'It depends'* and *'Just enough detail'*. Which means that uncertainty will be an inherent part of the story even before we start.

And whilst it does indeed solve real business-problems and the like, it's not a *'solution'* as such. Its not about *'problems'*, either, it's more about making sense of a context-space, within which that contrast between *'problem'* and *'solution'* is itself one of the key barriers against making sense.

The real core of it, perhaps, is about skills, about what skills are, why we need them, what happens in skills-development, and how development of skill is inherently different from training.

The crucial distinction between training and skills is in how they view the role of methods, the means via which action is taken and guided towards some desired outcome:

In training, methods are assumed to be context-independent, and that each method will lead always to the same outcomes, regardless of who or what applies that method. Because of this, everyone is taught the same method. In effect, method is the sole centre of focus, with context either ignored or seen as irrelevant.

In skills-based work, methods are assumed to be somewhat context-dependent, and that use of the same methods in different contexts may or will lead to different outcomes. Which means that different methods will likely need to be applied, dependent on the context, in order to achieve the equivalent outcome. Which means, in turn, that we can't just teach the same method in each case, because it may well work only with one person in one context. And that those that cannot adapt to the context, cannot be relied upon to deliver the desired outcomes.

In effect, the appropriate method to use in each context arises from a context specific mix of *'objective'* and *'subjective'* factors, respectively the *'constraints'* and *'individual approaches'* in the context. So the key focus needs to be on those factors, rather than on specific methods that arise from them.

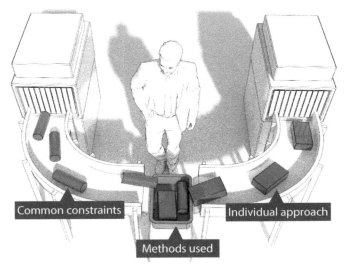

Two of the key factors affecting how an issue can be resolved.
*For example loading a passenger plane: **Common constraints** include aircraft*
*sizes and fuel requirements. **Individual approach** might be how a British*
airport loads passengers and luggage compared to an Australian airport.
*The **methods used** are a combination of both.*

In training, we push the predefined methods into someone or something, almost literally forcing them onto the same track of action, mindset and more. And because training is method-focused, the methods, by definition, are always *'right'*. Anyone or anything that does not achieve the desired outcome from that training is presumed to be *'wrong'* or *'at fault'*.

Ultimately, for skills-based methods, there's no such thing as *'right'* or *'wrong'*, just *'better'* or *'worse'* in terms of reaching towards desired-outcomes. And, crucially, working with the real-world takes priority over any predefined *'the method'*...

No doubt training is always the *'easiest'*-seeming option, and certainly the cheapest, which is one reason why it's so popular. But the reality is that, in the real-world, context is king, which is a key reason why training tends to work better in theory than it does in real-world practice.

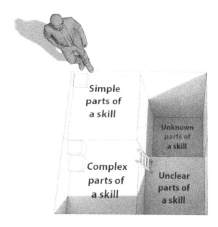

Classroom theory only covers parts of learning a skill, leaving the rest in the shadows.

In practice, and particularly so in a whole-context field such as EA, we need to cover the whole of the context space, not only the easy bit that can be addressed by training...

There is another side to this, about purpose, about desire, about what we want to do, rather than only what we can do. Linked to that are concerns such as competence, that the methods we use will change according to our experience and maturity within that skill. And, moving more to the *'constraints'* side, there are other *'external'* elements such as inherent-uncertainty.

So the methods we need in each context will depend not just on *constraints* and *individual* approaches, but on these broader *'external'* factors too. Below we see how these external factors interact with constraints and individual approaches.

This approach differs from some which focus on repeatable training for repeatable methods in repeatable contexts, while this approach focuses on individual-oriented understanding and skills to obtain context-specific methods for use in often either partially or wholly non-repeatable contexts.

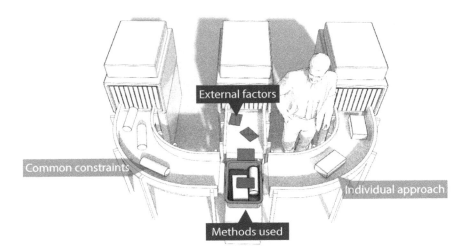

External factors can also affect how an issue can be resolved.
*Here we have added 'External factors' to 'Common constraints and 'Individual approaches'. For example loading a passenger plane: **External factors** might include how weather and geopolitics can shut down an entire airport. The **methods used** are a combination of all of the factors.*

6: Guiding the dance of change

How do we work with change?

How do we deal with change? Or cope with it?

Perhaps a better metaphor would be to dance with change.

That's not a new metaphor, of course: for business-change, for example, there's the now-classic book by Peter Sengé and others, *'The Dance of Change'*. But if it's a dance, then what are the steps for that dance? How do we do that dance? And how do we get others to join with us in that dance?

Working with change is a continuing dance of sense, make-sense, decide and act, then sense and make-sense again from the actions we've just done. And within that overall dance of exploration, there are the same distinct two alternating phases: a period when everything flows, when we seem to know exactly what to do, and to do next; and a period when we lose the flow, where nothing seems to work, and there's a risk that everything will come to a grinding halt. When we lose the flow in *'the dance of change'*, we need to fall back to a known base-pattern for exploration.
The Five Elements tool helps show this:

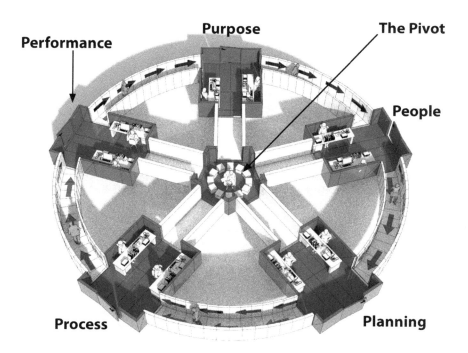

A simplified version of the Five Elements tool.

In any work on change, we'd be likely to use a wide variety of check-lists and other tools to guide the exploration, particularly in the *'make-sense'* part in that cycle of of the *'sense/make-sense/decide/act'*. In practice, there could be an infinite variety of tools we might use: which is a huge challenge in keeping track of where we are at each moment in the exploration, in the dance, and of how to move between tools and link the tools together.

For our own work on tools-for-change, we resolve this challenge by a simple mechanism of keywords: if a keyword or key-phrase comes up in the dialogue of exploration, that in turn acts as a cue to suggest a tool we might turn to at that point. I use keywords associated with each tool, for exactly this purpose: for example, if the words *'opportunity'* or *'challenge'* came up in the conversation, that might suggest that we could turn to the **SCORE**[1] tool at that point, to explore the interplay of challenge, opportunity, risk, and the capabilities we'd need so as best to respond to each.

When we're well locked into that dance of change, then we'd swap between tools, bringing our insights back to the table to share with others as we need. In a sense, *Five Elements (see above)* isn't that important as such at that phase.

But when we lose the flow, that's when having something like Five Elements becomes really important: Five Elements provides a default fallback-pattern to keep us engaged in the dance of change. It can also represent typical departments within an organisation, in brief it covers:

1. **Purpose** (*'Why'*) Why are we doing this? What's the big-picture, the broader story? What are the core principles, the criteria for success?
2. **People** (*'Who'*) Who's involved? What are their needs, their responsibilities?
3. **Preparation** (*'How'*) How are we going to do this? What do we need to bring together to make this work?
4. **Process** (*'What / Where / When'*) What are we doing, right now? How are we resolving run-time uncertainties, right now?
5. **Performance** (*'Outcomes'*) What did we do? What benefits did we gain? How much did things work to plan? What do we learn from this, to do better next time?

There's a *pattern* to it, moving outward from the centre with a specific aim in mind, and then back to the centre again with the information gained through that move.

There's a *sequence* to it, a distinct set of steps moving from one focus to the next, and if we try to skip any of the steps, during this default-mode phase, we'll likely lose connection with the dance as a whole.

---

1. *A simplified version of the SCORE tool is shown in the book:*
   Tools for Change-mapping, *which is available on Amazon.*

There's a *rhythm* to it, out and back, steadily round and round, iteration after iteration, gathering new information as we go.

Round and round in that pattern, until the path returns. And we know when the path returns when we notice a cue-keyword that takes us off into a more-detailed space, and we then return back to that default Five Elements pattern again when we lose the path once more. All until we've done *'just enough'* of the dance, just enough exploration, and then turn to put into practice what we've learned in the dance. *(Which itself is all part of a larger dance, of course…)*

Providing consistent guidance and governance for the overall dance of change: that's the role of a core-level default-pattern such as Five Elements.

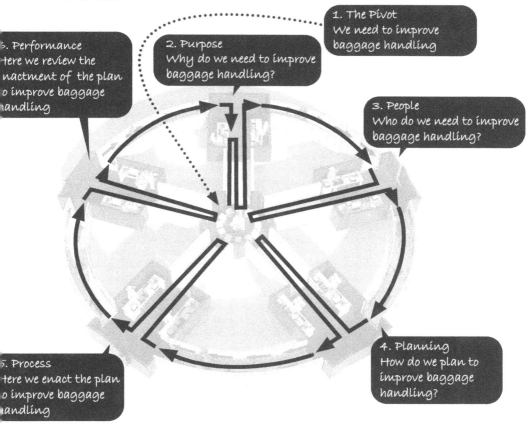

A simplified version of the Five Elements tool in use exploring how to improve baggage handling inside an airport. In this example we start at the 'pivot' and move around clockwise. Once we have done one cycle we can go round again, to improve further.

⬠⬠⬠⬠⬠ *Taken from the chapter:* **Guiding the dance of change**

7: Architecture as boxes, lines and glue

What do enterprise architects do? And why?

By far the most common metaphor is 'boxes and lines', or 'boxes and arrows'.

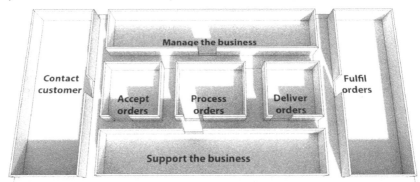

A typical diagram showing the key functions of an organisation

The 'boxes' that represent the various core functions of the organisation are all visible enough; yet the 'glue' that connects them, the spaces between the boxes, is much less self-evident, and we often have to make a deliberate effort to take notice of it. The 'glue', the "invisible stretchy stuff", is what holds together all of the 'boxes' that make up the activities of the organisation.

For some the organisation is an arrangement of boxes so stable and so perfectly interlocked that it needs no glue at all. Yet it's an aim that's simply not achievable in the present-day world: all of the boxes are changing in shape and size, all of the time, in response to real-world pressures, and all the nesting of boxes-within-boxes-within-boxes is changing all the time, too. Which means that, inevitably, there's a need for 'invisible stretchy stuff' to hold it all together. Which means there's a need for people who can work with this 'invisible stretchy stuff' that holds everything together.

Otherwise known as architects, the people who work **between** the boxes:

How analysts and enterprise architects examine an organisation

Who are also the people who work with the *'lines and arrows'* that connect between the boxes. Which suggests a richer metaphor for architecture: *Boxes, lines and glue.*
That's the metaphor that we need.

Architects often struggle to explain what it is that they do, and the business-value of what they do, the value-proposition for EA and the like. Part of the problem, of course, is that architects mostly work with that *'invisible stretchy stuff'*, in the *'invisible'* space between the boxes.
The point is we need both analysts and enterprise architects, to better help an organisation.

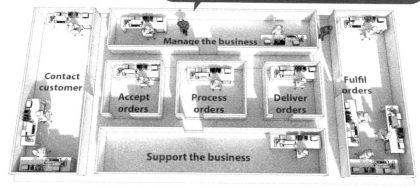

How analysts typically examine an organisation

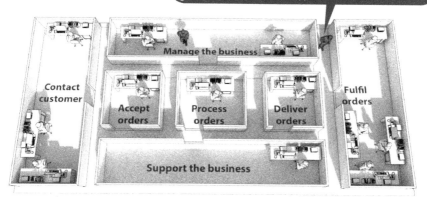

How enterprise architects typically examine an organisation

⬠⬠⬠⬠⬠ *Taken from the chapter:* **Architecture as boxes, lines and glue**

8: Business architecture and EA

What many people call 'enterprise-architecture' is actually a contraction of an older and more accurate term: 'enterprise-wide IT-architecture' (EWITA).

Which no doubt seems fair enough at first, after all, *'enterprise-architecture'* is a useful shorthand for EWITA. The catch is that that contraction becomes dangerously misleading when we move beyond an IT-only space, and outward towards the enterprise itself.

A common model called the *'BDAT-stack'* underpins many frameworks, looks upwards from the base of that stack of boxes *(see below).*

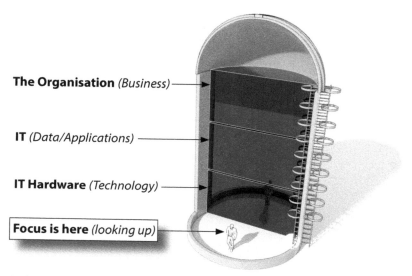

The Organisation *(Business)*

IT *(Data/Applications)*

IT Hardware *(Technology)*

Focus is here *(looking up)*

A typical Business, Data, Application and Technology (BDAT) stack model

A BDAT-type stack's focus is whatever is at the base of the stack. For BDAT itself, that's IT-hardware. We cannot run a BDAT-stack backwards. A common mistake that is made that one assumes we can start anywhere in the stack, but if we do that from anywhere other than the base, the result gives us a scope that can be *(and usually is)* dangerously incomplete.

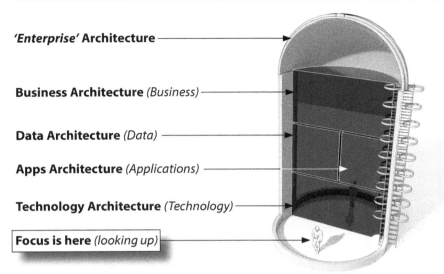

'Enterprise' Architecture

Business Architecture *(Business)*

Data Architecture *(Data)*

Apps Architecture *(Applications)*

Technology Architecture *(Technology)*

Focus is here *(looking up)*

A BDAT stack too focused on IT

This is what the classic BDAT-based *'enterprise'*-architecture frameworks tell us is the full scope of EA *(see above)*. The catch, as shown, is that a BDAT-type stack always start from the base, in this case, focussed on Technology Architecture, the architecture for IT-hardware.
Which means that, by definition, such *'EA'*-frameworks can meaningfully answer only one business-question: *"What is the most appropriate way to organise our IT-hardware?"*

We need to remember that there's a lot more involved than just the business itself, we need to explore and understand the context for that business. In other words, the architecture of the shared-enterprise within which that business will operate *(see below)*.

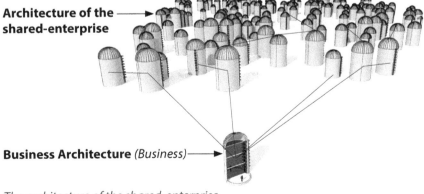

Architecture of the shared-enterprise

Business Architecture *(Business)*

The architecture of the shared-enterprise

⬠⬠⬠⬠⬠ *Taken from the chapter:* **On business-architecture and enterprise-architecture**

9: How do we make sense of EA?

***The concept of 'whole-enterprise architecture' connects with a fair
few people***, particularly those who've some experience of systems-thinking,
design-thinking and so on. But others are still unsure. How do we bring
those different worlds together, so that we can put these ideas to
practical use? How do we make it make sense?

Part of the problem is the age-old clash between theory and practice.
Practice needs theory; theory needs practice. Practitioners tend to be
wary of too much theory. People simply don't have time to stop and
think about theory. Yet the fact that they don't look enough to theory may
itself be a key reason why they don't have the time…

Chicken and egg: which comes first, theory or practice? How do we get out
of that loop?

There's also the *"in a perfect world"* excuse, as my colleague mentioned the
other day:

*"It's just chaos out there, doing everything the hard way. But if I suggest
anything to cut down on the chaos, even something really simple like using
scripts in a spreadsheet, so that they could get a chance to get started, it's
always the same response: "yes, in a perfect world, but…", "that might work in a
perfect world, but…", "we could do that in a perfect world, but in the
real world…".*

What's worrying was that this was the architects, the people who were
supposed to understand IT-architecture. Worse, he said, they were hardly
using any of their architecture tools to clean up the architecture: in fact, of
the thousand licences for a high-end EA tool-set that their corporation had
paid for, they were actually using just six.

Making sense of the enterprise
A quick summary of some of the main parts we need to make sense of:

• it's about the architecture of the enterprise as a whole, how everything
  works together towards some overall aim
• it's about the underlying *'why'* of the overall enterprise, and how that links
   to the *'how'* and *'with-what'* and so on that make everything happen
• it's about both structure and story, in the broadest sense of each
• it's planning for and working with change, with inherent uncertainty,
  rather than trying to fight against it
• it's about identifying and managing hidden costs and risks, and hidden
  opportunities too
• it includes a strong focus on where people fit within the overall enterprise

- it's about defining and using tool-sets, visualisations, dashboards and other techniques to help people make sense of what's happening within the enterprise, and in making decisions about how to keep the enterprise on track
- it's about bringing all of these themes down into really practical, concrete, everyday expression, enhancing effectiveness through the enterprise

All straightforward and obvious. Also straightforward and obvious, is that lack of awareness and integration of these themes is a large part of why there's so much stress at work and elsewhere.

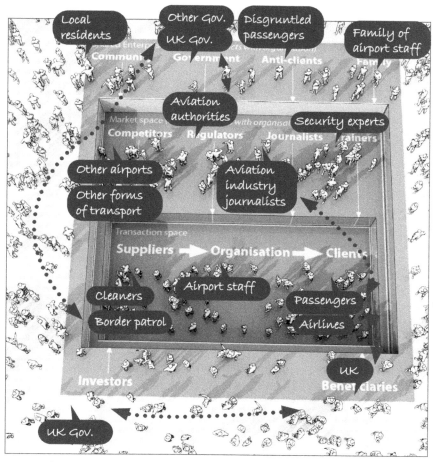

A simplified version of the Whole EA tool can be used to better understand the people who are directly or indirectly part of an enterprise, such as improving an airport. You can also start to see connections between each of the groups (dotted lines).

Taken from the chapter: **How do we make EA make sense?**

10: The glue between strategy and execution

A strategy is a statement of intent that something should happen.

Execution is what is actually done to make that intent actually happen.

The reality is that there may be many disconnects between strategy and execution. These potential disconnects typically increase with scope, scale and complexity. In practice, and especially in large complex organisations, it may be very difficult to execute a chosen strategy.

One reason is that an organisation brings together many different disciplines, each of which have their own terminology, their own context-specific experience. *'Translation'*-difficulties are very common between disciplines and even between work-teams. Another reason is that organisations tend to be structured in silos, again reinforcing barriers of *'language'*, but also providing all manner of other boundaries of politics, control, authority, hierarchy and the like. Larger corporations may also have to deal with multiple jurisdictions, multiple natural-languages, multiple human-cultures and so on, all of which add their own difficulties for translation and execution, especially where the strategy requires context specific forms of execution.

Another reason is that different departments may well be going through different changes, and/or different rates of change. Maintaining alignment over time across all of the disparate departments will rarely be simple.

Yet another reason is the translation from abstract to concrete, from strategic vision to real-world practice. The use of a well-worn phrase, *the devil is in the details*, details which may not have been allowed for in the initial strategy.

As a result of these and other related forces and constraints, the organisation has a natural tendency to fragmentation. There is therefore a need for a distinct discipline responsible for bridging all of the gaps, aiding communication, providing advice on design within and between departments, and generally assisting in both the execution of strategy and in formulating strategy.

By convention, a role that is responsible for linking between departments in this way and for this purpose is referred to as an *'architect'*.

In a small organisation, it is usually possible for one person to cover all of the *'architect'* role. In principle, this is the responsibility of the CEO or equivalent, but in practice the role will often be delegated to others.

As the scope, scale and complexity grow, this *'architecture'* responsibility will usually be partitioned amongst more and more people, each covering different aspects of the overall scope, and with different balance between depth *(specialism)* and breadth *(generalism)*.

Depth is needed in order to grasp the detail needed to achieve execution.

Breadth is needed to ensure that each department and sub-department and project links cleanly and appropriately with others.

We could summarise *depth* as follows:

• *none*: the other department is considered out-of-scope, not relevant or non-existent

• *black-box*: the other department is known only in terms of its exposed connection or exchange points, without requiring any knowledge of the department's internal operation

• *white-box*: some knowledge of the other department's internals, sufficient for concerns such as cross-department trade-offs, probability and direction of change, failure scenarios and risks, disaster-recovery scenarios and options, etc

• *full-depth*: full knowledge and experience of the other department, to an identifiable level of skill *(e.g. Trainee, Apprentice, Journeyman, Master)*

The translation from abstract to concrete
We could summarise levels of abstraction with the Zachman layers[1], from row one *(business context, within which the strategy will operate)* to row five *(action-plan immediately prior to execution)*.

We could summarise scope *(and therefore **breadth**)* in terms of the various departments, sub-departments and silos of the organisation and its business context. The precise list will depend on industry, organisation-structure and many other factors, but common examples are indicated by responsibilities of the respective senior executive:
CFO *(finance and 'business of business')*, CIO *(information)*, COO *(operations)*, CTO (technology), CKO *(knowledge/learning)* and so on. As above, the CEO has responsibility for the architectural integration of the organisation as a whole.

Each architect-role will have its own distinct combination of scope, scale, complexity, abstraction, depth and breadth.

---

1. The Zachman framework
Uses layers to help understand what needs to happen at each stage of a change.

Note that even in the same scope, architects may have different requirements for depth or breadth. For example, a process-automation architect may regard power-supply and skill-sets as out-of-scope *('none'-depth)*, whereas an architect working on disaster-recovery planning would need *'white-box'* depth in each of those *'out-of-scope'* areas.

To identify the required responsibility, authority, reporting-relationships and the like, it will be useful to categorise these roles according to Len Fehskens' outline, where italic lower case *'x'* means the provisional role, such as data architect:

- **xA** *(e.g. data-architect, Siebel architect, brand-architect)*: architect within department or narrower scope *(sub-department, portfolio, project)*; usually row-3 to row-5 *(see below)* with limited breadth; usually *'black-box'* or no depth in departments outside of their own immediate scope
- **ExA** *(e.g. enterprise IT-architect, enterprise business-architect, enterprise security-architect)*: an architect across a complete department; usually row-2 to row-4, but they may need to do deep-dive in their own department; usually *'white-box'* or *'black-box'* depth in departments outside of their own scope
- **EA** *(enterprise-architect)*: architect across all departments; usually row-1 to row-3, but may need to do deep-dive *in* any department; they must have some level of *'white-box'* depth across all departments

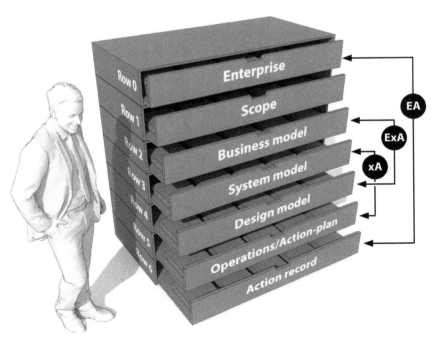

A simplified version of the Zachman framework

11: Two roles for Enterprise Architects

The internal enterprise-architect and the external enterprise-architect.

There are two radically different roles for enterprise-architects:

• the **internal** enterprise-architect
• the **external** enterprise-architect

They're both focused on *'the architecture of the enterprise'*, but it's important not to mix them up, because they require different temperaments and different approaches to business-relationships.

The **internal enterprise-architect** is actively responsible for the *'enterprise DNA'* of a single organisation. They typically either report direct to the CEO *(who has the ultimate authority and responsibility for that 'DNA', but in practice probably doesn't have the time to do much about it)*, or else are attached to the CEO Office or a senior-level strategy-group.
The key point here is that, to use Kevin Smith's term, this enterprise-architect role acts as *"the glue between strategy and execution".* Which means that they need direct person-to-person relations with people at all levels and in all departments of the organisation and enterprise. Developing these relationships takes time, often ten or more years in a typical large organisation. So the best people for this kind of role are those who have *"come up through the ranks"* and built a personal network on the way. The CEO can and should do the enterprise-architect role for a start-up, but once the organisation grows beyond about a dozen people the role will typically need to be part of someone else's explicit responsibilities.
This role is about how the idea of EA, that *"things work better when they work together, with efficiency, with elegance, on purpose, in practice"*, is expressed throughout this organisation, in terms of its business-purpose.

The **external enterprise-architect** *(or consultant enterprise-architect)* is actively responsible for promoting the *'idea'* and practice of EA itself. It's important that they maintain their independence as much as practicable, though for practical reasons many will work as part of a consulting-organisation of some kind. Their person-to-person relations are with other architects, again in many different departments and at all levels, but across many different organisations and enterprise-types.

Their primary role is *practice-refresh*[1] for in-house enterprise-architects: they help to keep the overall architecture up-to-date on methods, practices, and frameworks, and help to lift the *architecture-maturity*[2] and *architecture-capability*[3] of the internal team.

They also act as external peer-review, to reduce the risk of an insular and often destructive *'group-think'*[4] developing within an organisation. This role too requires many years of experience, but this experience will have been gained across multiple disciplines in multiple organisations and, preferably, multiple industries.

The internal enterprise-architect deals with architecture in **depth**; the external enterprise-architect deals with architecture in **breadth**. An organisation's architecture gains most from an appropriate balance of these two roles, not one or the other, but always some of both.

The worst possible combination of these two roles is unfortunately that which many large consultancies try to promote: full long-term control of an organisation's enterprise-architecture by an external consultancy. An enterprise-architecture works right at the core of an organisation and enterprise: so assigning responsibility for the organisation's DNA to an external party is not a good idea…

---

1. Practice refresh
Examining how enterprise architecture is performed currently and if there are new approaches which may improve its effectiveness.

2. Architecture-maturity
A measure of your capability in terms of EA. Being able to do certain tasks within EA.

3. Architecture-capability
What you can do with your architecture, including what you can change and what you can work with.

4. Group-think
Where a group wanting to work well together, agree on everything without properly understanding everything.

 Taken from the chapter: **Two roles for enterprise-architects**

12: Analyst, anarchist, architect

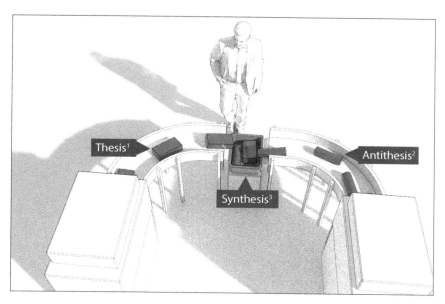

A simplified version of a logical model some attribute to Hegel
1. Thesis (theory)
2. Antithesis (contradiction to theory)
3. A combination of thesis and antithesis

Thesis, antithesis, synthesis: the old Hegelian triad (a simplified version is shown above). But what's that got to do with enterprise-architecture and the like? Quite a lot, as it happens, though we might need to take a detour or two to get there, of course!

In brief, the *antithesis* is not a contradiction of the *thesis*, but a challenge to the assumptions on which the thesis is based, which then leads to a *synthesis* that makes real practical sense. And that starts to look a lot more like enterprise-architecture.

Or, more precisely, in the business context, the three distinct roles of business-analyst, business-anarchist, and enterprise-architect. Which might need a bit more explanation.

The **business-analyst** role is well-understood, I think. That's the 'thesis' part of the triad, the Abstract, the Immediate. As the name suggests, it's all about analysis, often about what can be seen in 'the Now', about order, certainty, honing the algorithms, defining the 'best-practice' methods for making decisions. It's very good at enhancing efficiency through careful calculation; very good at doing things right.

The catch is that the real world is not just about efficiency, nor only about doing things right: it's also about *doing the right things*, about bringing it all together to enhance overall *effectiveness*.

And with analysis alone, it's all too easy to create something that is extremely efficient at going off at full-tilt but in the wrong direction, which, in terms of its *effectiveness (or lack of it)*, can easily be worse than doing nothing at all.

Which is why analysis alone is not enough.

Which is why we need those other two roles: the anarchist, and the enterprise architect.

The **business-anarchist** role is perhaps the least-understood of the three, certainly the least-popular, anyway. It's the *'antithesis'* part of the triad, the Negative, but also the Mediated. One of the key problems for analysis is that it's entirely dependent on its assumptions: everything within that frame of assumptions would be valid enough if the assumptions are correct, yet analysis has no means *within itself* to test those assumptions, and make sure that they do indeed align with the real world of *"trial, error and experience"*. If no-one is willing to question the assumptions, or even admit that they *are* just assumptions, things can increase in risk, or worse, very quickly indeed…

That's a crucial problem there, right at the core of all analysis; yet unfortunately it's one that's evaded all too often in a business context. And that's especially true where the drive for *'efficiency'* is allowed to override everything else. So if we're going to get things to work well in the real world, we *need* some definite means to face those often rather unpalatable facts. And that's where the *business-anarchist* role comes into the picture.

It's an extremely important role, and also an extremely responsible one, too: namely, *challenge every assumption*. It's about challenging, but it's not negative, not merely challenging for the sake of challenging: it's about creating space for mediation, for sense-making in a deeper, more directed sense. It's not just about doing things right, but also about being sure that we're *doing the right things*, too, making sure that every assumption has a solid basis, so that the analysts can do their job well.

And the **enterprise-architect** role is about bringing it all together again. It's the *'synthesis'* part of the triad; but it's also about the Concrete, about making things real, being *effective*, about *doing the right things right* in a concrete, practical way. It's about bringing things together such that everything works well together, responsive to change as required, and as a unified whole.

Where the analyst takes things apart, and the anarchist takes apart the thinking that takes things apart, the architect brings everything together again, by resolving the fragmentation in new, more effective ways.

Some people seem to think that the enterprise-architect role is rather abstract. But it's not abstract at all, because the architect is responsible for bringing everything in scope to real, usable, useful completion in the real world. It's not abstract: in many ways it's perhaps the most concrete that anything can get.

And yes, it does indeed all start from the abstract.

Yet the point here is that this is also a triad: thesis, antithesis, synthesis; analyst, anarchist, architect. None of these roles stands alone: each depends on each of the others, always in dynamic tension with each other, dynamic balance: *"the Concrete, the Synthesis, the Absolute, must always pass through the phase of the Negative, that is, Mediation"*. And yet they're also distinct and often very different roles.

One way to resolve the architecture of that architecture is to have just one person doing all of those roles, after all, they're different roles, not necessarily different people. But that can sometimes be quite a *'big ask'*, because each of the roles does demand different skill-sets, different methods, even different world views. But there are many different ways to do it, of course: *"whatever works"* is probably the best guideline here.

In a small organisation that has only a small pool of specialist staff, we might not have much choice, because there simply aren't enough people around to do all the roles required. By contrast, in a large organisation, we might well have the luxury to have separate jobs for separate roles. But whichever way we do it, we have to make sure that all three roles are adequately covered, are adequately supported, and that they do indeed work together in a unified way.

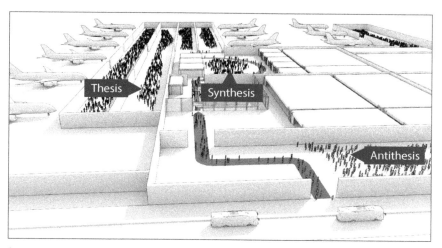

Large organisations can have teams of people who will produce thesis, antithesis and synthesis.

⬠⬠⬠⬠⬠ *Taken from the chapter: **Analyst, anarchist, architect***

13: Applied-scientist or alchemist?

Is enterprise-architecture more akin to alchemy than applied-science?
And if so, what would this imply to how we study, discuss, teach, learn and
apply enterprise-architectures in real-world practice?

Some lessons we can learn from the past include:

Alchemy Lesson #1 might be plain old health-and-safety, of course. If we're
going to be mucking around with things that, metaphorically speaking, can
go off *'BANG!'* in our faces, it's wise to have a fair idea of how to handle it…
But it is difficult to get that *'fair idea of how to handle it'* when everything's
unique and people are being secretive about it all. Somehow, we have
to get it over to people that they need to tell us about anything that's a
potential hazard, and that includes things that can be hazardous in
not-so-obvious ways, such as at risk of damaging trust.

Alchemy Lesson #2 is about use of patterns or metaframeworks[1], rather
than predefined *'recipes'*. We need to work with the uniqueness, rather than
pretend that it doesn't exist, and patterns provide us with a means to bridge
between repeatability and uniqueness. In a sense, our equivalents of the old
alchemists' classics are the frameworks we know. The catch is that we need
to think of them more as patterns, not *'frameworks'*: whenever we
use them, we need to keep the focus on *'adapt, then adopt'*.

Alchemy Lesson #3 is about the real need for precise, disciplined
observation. What we're really aiming for here is a continuous, overarching
sense of the whole as whole, a knowing of where the fine-detail matters,
and where it doesn't. This is about more than just looking, more than just
digital-information: often it requires embracing using all of our senses.

We don't get this from studying just the theory, if we get too hung up on
theory, and deviate too far from real-world practice, that's when
things go badly wrong. Perhaps the most important thing here is to notice
things that don't fit our expectations, they're often very easy to miss,
especially given Gooch's Paradox, that *"Things not only have to be seen to
believed, but also have to be believed to be seen"*.

Alchemy Lesson #4 is that we need to work consistently, to allow time for
things to mature. For EA, the key point here is that little to no real value
will be delivered if we treat the development of the architecture as
a *'one-off project'*. Instead, it is about real-world practice, day after
day, month after month, year after year, working with the whole-as-whole.

---

1. Metaframework
A generic template to make other frameworks.

Alchemy Lesson #5 is about *'just enough documentation'*. In a sense, *'just enough documentation'*, or Just Enough Detail. We need enough documentation and detail to keep our finger on the pulse, but not so much as to slow us down. It is a tricky balance…

One of the reasons it's tricky is because of Lesson #4, about working consistently over long periods of time, certainly for years, quite possibly for decades. Over those kinds of time-scales, memory alone will not suffice: we're going to need to write it down, or document it in some other way. And in ways that we can still access and search years or decades later, which in these current times of rapid obsolescence is not as as easy as it might at first seem.

We also need to remember that whilst scribbled sketch notes might well be adequate if it's just for ourselves, and just for a handful of years at most, it definitely won't be enough if it's across an entire enterprise or industry, and over decades or more. That's where the theme of patterns comes into the story: it's often a lot easier to document the adaptation of a pattern, than trying to document everything. Yet it's also where we come across the next *'lesson from alchemy'*…

Alchemy Lesson #6 is that some secrecy is often unavoidable, and even necessary. Every trade has its own *'trade-secrets'*; most businesses have some kind of *'secret sauce'* behind their story *(or would like to have such, anyway)*. And there are often very good reasons for this, beyond just protecting and privatising a source of monetary income: for example, many disciplines are just too dangerous, in many different senses, to risk making everything fully open.

Some find that making things cryptic is a way of slowing people down *'just enough'* whilst they develop the basic skills and their own essential safe-practices. We still see the same in present-day health-and-safety hazard-management: we don't let first-level apprentices play around with power-tools, for example, let alone poisons or explosives.

And some contexts require a subtle form of secrecy just to do their job. In one organisation, I have seen coded tags for client-records which might seem innocuous-enough on the surface, but actually act as warnings to the initiated: *'VIP'*, for example, which meant *'difficult customer'*. In each of those cases, it was a simple form of protection against lawsuits and suchlike, in case the record needed to be shown to the client under Freedom Of Information laws, but no doubt you'll have much the same in many other places and contexts in your own organisation and beyond. Secrecy for its own sake is a nuisance, or worse, but there are times where it is essential: so in our enterprise-architectures, we'll need not only to document and support those cases, but also why they're needed.

⬠⬠⬠⬠⬠ *Taken from the chapter:* **Enterprise-architect-applied-scientist, or alchemist?**

14: EA and solution-architecture

What are the respective roles of EA and solution-architecture?
How do they relate with respect to each other, and with respect, too?

As an enterprise-architect, I deal mainly with issues that straddle across the whole enterprise-space, with an emphasis on breadth;
the solution-architect maintains the breadth pertinent to a specific scope, but also focusses right down on the technical and other detail needed for that specific solution.
In a sense, EA is more about context, SA is more about content.

To give a concrete example, imagine we're working for a large airport that wants to save money, yet that wants to make those savings sustainable in the long-term, by building and leveraging mutual trust. In the broadest sense with customers, suppliers, employees, investors and so on.

One practical way they can do this is with self-insurance of their buildings. They don't have an external insurer, they just deal with the incident straight away, whatever it costs, and without any argument. Which actually ends up much cheaper and much quicker all round, and everyone's a lot less hassled and a lot more happy about what is otherwise a rather unhappy kind of incident. It also builds trust, lots of it. Yet it also depends on trust, likewise lots of it. Which means that we can't tackle it as if it's just a *'quick money saver'*, it's a fundamental shift in the overall architecture of the enterprise.

To make it work, as an architect, I'm going to need an **architecture of trust** that supports that fundamental shift in attitude across the enterprise, which in turn will depend on a lot of other more tangible changes to underpin that shift. One of those changes is that we will need a much better handle on some types of information, because claims-incidents, costs-savings, customer-reputation and supplier-relations all become so intertwined that in effect they can almost become proxies for each other.
To make sense of that, and to enable appropriate real-time choices at every level from executive to operations, we're going to need some kind of *'trust-dashboard'*, where all these information-themes come together.
Yet its design and implementation will also need to be able to handle a lot of change, because there's a lot of wicked-problems and subtle problems hiding in there; and we're going to need a fair amount of rethink, probably over several years, before we could settle on something that is self-adapting enough to work well.

As an enterprise-architect, I have a fair idea about what's needed for this *'trust-dashboard'*, but I don't know how to do it. Not in enough detail to make it work well in the real-world, anyway. *(That's Step 1: admit that I don't know how to do it…)*

But to use the old quote, *"I know someone who does".* *(That's Step 2: build and maintain a good professional-network across a range of people that's much broader than just my immediate peers.)* And there are at least two people I need to know in this case: a *domain-architect*[1], who understands the broader information-technology issues and the way the technology trends are going; and a *solution-architect*[2] who knows what works in *this* organisation's technology and culture.

To do my part of this job properly, I have to be able to build a rough concept of this *'information-dashboard'* that's both detailed-enough and credible enough for those people to say *"We can see what you're getting at, but, you know, we'd be better if we did it this way. And anyway that technology will soon be obsolete, so you need this new approach instead".* And I would say, kind of, sort of, yes, but I need it to do that thing, for this reason, and not force people too much along this path, because of that thing, and so on. Back and forth we go, bouncing off each each other's perspectives as we iterate towards a workable idea. *(That's Step 3: the real core of architecture is the conversations, the detail is the outcome of those conversations.)*

This is only going to work if there's strong mutual respect between us. *(That's Step 4: build and maintain strong work-relations with my professional contacts)* I need to listen to the domain-architect and solution architect: they know their job far better than I do, and far better than I ever will, so I need to respect that fact, and respect their knowledge too. *(Which in part depends on Step 1: knowing that I don't know, and hence being respectful enough to ask for advice…)* And it's also up to me to gain their trust enough that they don't dismiss me as some kind of ivory-tower airhead who's just there to waste their time, that I'm dealing with a broader scope that extends beyond their domain, but I need their help within their domain. *(That's Step 5: know what my domain is and isn't, what I do know as well as what I don't, and where and how it overlaps with others'.)*

Which is where, eventually, we get down to the detail of *'backbone versus edge*[3]*'*. Here we explore detailed IT requirements of the organisation in stages, starting only with the items we *must* have in common. We start with the bare minimum, and build it so that it's *(re)*usable anywhere, and extensible for any purpose. The key point is that we need to keep awareness always on the underlying requirement, rather than solely on any specific implementation of that need.

---

1. Domain architect
Has a focus on a particular specialism such as data.
2. Solution architects
Tackle all of the issues to do with change projects.
3. Backbone and edge is discussed in more detail overleaf.

That's the kind of conversation I would need to build and maintain with those people, regarding IT. Yet as a broad-scope enterprise-architect, I'd also need to build and maintain similar conversations with their counterparts in fleet-operations, process-design, the finance space, Health & Safety and so on. I would also need to facilitate good conversations between them and IT as needed, too. It's a much broader scope: but because it's a broader scope, we enterprise-architects do not have the time or the knowledge to do all of the architecture ourselves, which is why we need good relations with the people who do.

IT-architecture focusses on information; enterprise-architecture also needs to include the physical 'things', the business-relations, the 'purpose'-type issues such as brands and reputation, and so on.
But whichever way we look at it, and whatever scope we need, all of it is architecture, it's all the same basic idea, really.

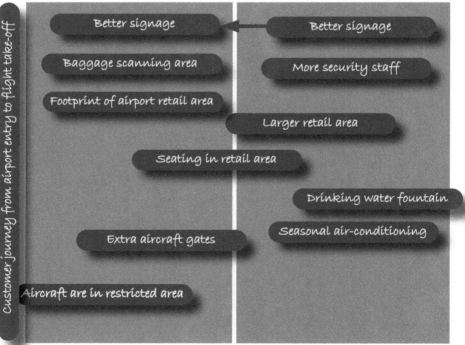

A simplified version of the Backbone and Edge tool. Here we explore some of the areas of an airport that cannot be changed (Backbone) and those that could (Edge). Sometimes these cross over as what might seem to be 'low impact', might (once thought about in more depth) cause major issues. For example, signage might seem easy to change, but if done incorrectly can cause many issues.

⬠⬠⬠⬠⬠ *Taken from the chapter:* **Linking enterprise-architecture with solution-architecture**

15: What futurists do, and why

Futurists build tools to help people better survive the future.
That's one of the key distinctions between **prediction** and **futures**.
The purpose of **prediction** is to provide a form of pseudo-certainty in a
context where, by definition, no true certainty can ever be had.
And prediction is easy: all you need do is to guess, perhaps even do a survey
to link the guess to an opinion-poll, and wrap it up in a palatable guise.
By contrast, **futures** is radically different. For a start, notice the plural: *futures*,
not the supposedly-singular *'the future'*. The purpose of futures is to help
people work with the uncertainties of the future, not pretend that those
uncertainties don't exist. And futures-work is hard, not least because, again,
it doesn't pretend that those uncertainties don't exist.
*As an aside, notice how often someone will ask you for an opinion or prediction
about the future, and then issue some kind of demand for 'proof' that that
assumed future is 'the truth'? All that they've proved is that they just don't get it:
the only way to 'prove' a future is to be there, experiencing it. At which point, of
course, it isn't 'the future': it's 'now'...]*

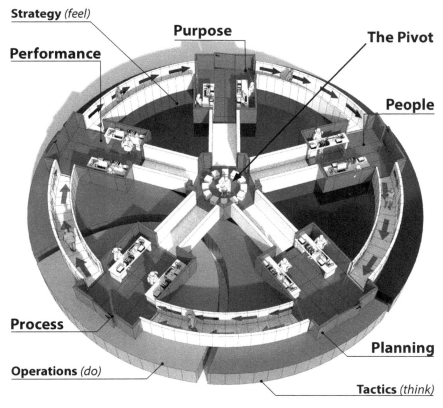

The cycle of change, from concept to production. For example if an airport
needed to improve baggage handling, there would be three main areas:
Strategy, Tactics and Operations. Underpinning the five elements, shown earlier.

So in part, the focus on tools: we create *'the future'* by literally creating it. From nowhere, from nothing, from out of thin air, whilst standing on top of what we already have.

The other huge complication here is that there's a fundamental difference between futures-work for far-future versus near-future.

Near-futures work is well within the normal time-scales of whatever it is that we're working with: it's just preparation for the next stage of action. The time-scales can vary quite a lot, depending on what it is that we're doing. The *'preparation'* time-scale for a forest or a vast energy-infrastructure project would be what many technology-businesses would consider so long-term as to be way out of sensible out of scope. But in essence, in each case, it's actually quite easy, because it's mostly just projection forward from *'the now'*, like prediction, but with more honesty and without all the marketing hype.

Far-futures work is more about *purpose*, the purpose of the enterprise, in its broadest sense. It sometimes looks much the same as near-futures work, and does use some of the same techniques, but in practice it's very different. Another difference is that it deals with every time-scale, all interleaving through each other. Sometimes we had to work in time-scales so far in the future that in the end, we just have to give up, tag the requirement as *'non-compliant'*, and had to leave it as a hope that someone in some none-too-distant future can find a way to make it work.

In our defence, what we did do was mark it explicitly as *'Needs Future Attention'*: we didn't just shove it into the *'too-hard basket'* and pretend that the problem no longer exists, as near-futures futurists sometimes do. Thus, however, we build up more and more debt for future generations to handle on our behalf, an all-too-literal form of theft from the future…

On occasion, the timelines may well stretch as far into the past as into the future.

Some things are predictable, in a way: you can argue with people, but you can't argue with physics, however impossible and *'unfair'* it might seem at times, and trees will always take time to grow. There's an old farmer's adage that the best time to plant a fruit-tree is twenty years ago; the second-best time is now. **By creating tools and techniques, futurists plant metaphoric fruit-trees to feed people in the future.**

But again, remember the time-scales: different trees take different times before they're mature enough to bear fruit. A blueberry-bush may be productive in as little as a couple of years, but a peach tree takes more like twenty, and a walnut-tree closer to a hundred, whilst an oak-tree, for timber, the time is measured not even in decades, but in centuries. *Much the same applies to the tools that futurists create.*

At the next time-scale, it doesn't take much of a futurist's eye to realise that enterprise-architecture eventually must expand out to at least a whole-of-organisation scope at some stage, and ultimately all the way out to a true whole-of-enterprise or enterprise-of-enterprises scope. That's inevitable, inescapable: the fact is that even at the lowest, most technical level of an IT-infrastructure, it's still an inherent part of a larger system, within a larger system, within a larger system, so there's no way to get even the IT-infrastructure to work properly unless we do acknowledge the literally all-inclusive nature of that system-of-systems.

The problem is it takes time for things to come to fruition.
Which, unfortunately, is where we hit up against the deadliest trap for all futures-work: thinking that near-futures and far-futures are the same, not least because that seemingly allows us to sidestep the concept stage. We see this trap in almost every business, especially those driven by the so-called *'need'* to satisfy the short-term view of the stock-market.

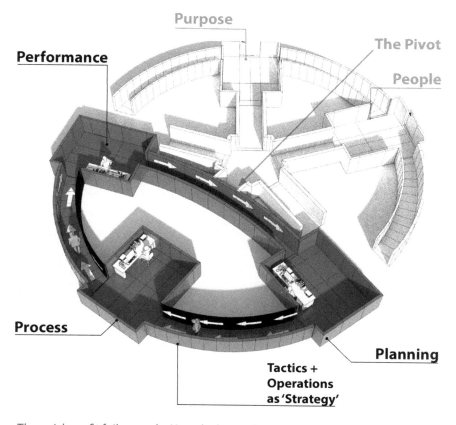

*The quick profit failure cycle. Here the basic **Five Elements** model (shown earlier) has cut off **Purpose** and **People**. Note also the doors in each room, which were open, are now also closed off, leading to more inward looking approaches.*

Whenever we pretend that near-futures is far-futures, that the distant future must, by definition, be exactly the same as today *(only somehow 'better', in some carefully ill-described way…)*, what we end up with, automatically, is what we might describe as the *'Quick-Profit Failure Cycle' (see last page)*. In a business-context, it's also known as *'grab the money and run'*: it looks like it works really well, in fact even more profitable because you don't have the *'overhead'* of anything that doesn't contribute to immediate profit.

But over the longer-term, which in some cases, especially with online-startups, is a *'long-term'* that can be measured in mere weeks, it will always collapse into a non-recoverable heap of metaphoric rubble, and almost always apparently *'without warning'.*

Why? How? Very simple: and entirely predictable, too. If you cut the real cycle short, it runs faster, yes, but you lose trust, you lose purpose, you lose connection with vision and value, you lose connection with people, and eventually you even lose the policies, the short-term reason for doing anything. Just one glance at that diagram above should tell you that the whole thing will inevitably spiral into the ground, sooner or later, and more likely sooner than later.

Our entire economics, for the past five thousand years, has restructured itself around exactly that type of flaw. The only way it's been able to prevent imploding is because of a myth of infinite-growth, literally consuming everything in its path, faster and faster and faster. But, again, you can't argue with physics: it is not possible to have infinite growth on a finite planet.

Which is why we need to work on alternatives, right here, right now. They might not seem urgent, right here, right now: but it'll take so long to get those alternatives into fruition that in practice it most definitely is urgent, right here, right now.

Yet notice that this becomes obvious, as soon as we extend the implications of that diagram up to a global scale.

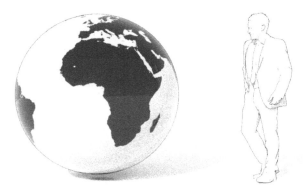

○○○○○ *Taken from the chapter:* **What futurists do, and why**

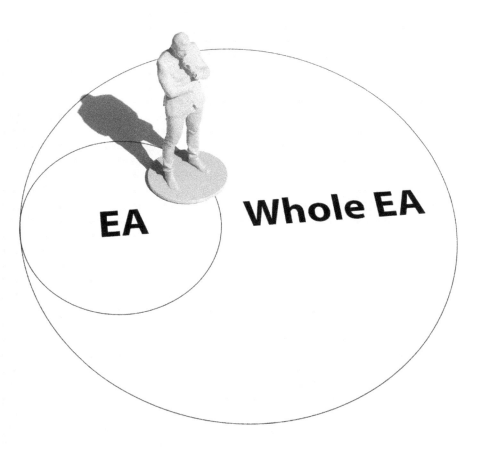

Part 2:

Enterprise Architecture basics

This section of the book is an abridged version of
'More basics for EA'
www.leanpub.com/tp-more-eabasics

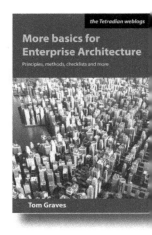

16: Keeping EA simple

Architecture: it's about structure, creating structures that people use. So any definition we develop about architectures is going to be something about structure, and about people. *(Technology enables architecture, but is not architecture itself: a rather important distinction…)*

Enterprise: it's not a business, it's a *commitment*. It's about emotion, feeling and so on. In practice, at a collective level, it's about how people come together to share their aims, and ways to achieve those shared aims. So enterprise-architecture is about the structures that people use to achieve their aims. Enterprise provides the *'Why'* for what we do and how we do it.

Business is part of that: people do business with each other as a way to achieve their respective aims. So *business-architecture[1] is about the structures that people use to do business with each other*, in support of their aims. Markets are obvious examples of structures that provide common space to do business; the law of contract is another kind of structure in that space; likewise exchange-mechanisms such as *fiat-currency[2] (money)* and credit-cards, and social structures such as the *'investor/beneficiary'* model that underpins so many commercial organisations. For an organisation, we could also say that its business-architecture is the architecture of *'the business of the business'*. And since it's about how we achieve aims, clearly it comes under the overall umbrella of enterprise-architecture.

Security is about feeling safe. So, in an organisational sense, *security architecture[3]* is about the structures that people use in order to feel safe whilst achieving their aims. For an organisation, clearly that too is part of its enterprise-architecture, but that is at right-angles to its business-architecture. In other words, architectures are not necessarily *'layered'*, but intersect as a kind of multi-layered, multi-faceted Venn diagram.

Brands denote stories; likewise for other symbols of that kind. Within an enterprise-architecture and a business-architecture, but not necessarily in a layered way, as such, a brand-architecture is about the structure of how stories link people with their aims. The enterprise is a story: brands and the like form a key part of how we create that story. Brand-architectures are primarily enclosed within our business-architecture, but may well extend beyond: from the perspective of the shared-enterprise, for example, we are custodians of a brand, not the *'possessors'* of it.

---

1. Business architecture
The structure and story of how the business works as a business.
2. Fiat currency
A type of currency that is not backed by a commodity, such as gold.
3. Security architecture
The structure and story of how to manage all aspects of security across a whole enterprise or business.

Processes are descriptions of what we do, in what sequence, and so on. They are the *'How'* of what we do. So *process-architecture*[1] is about the structures of how people organise what they do to achieve their aims. Notice that this doesn't exactly specify the *'How'* of the *'how'*: it could be people, IT, machines, or any combinations of those. *('Application-architecture*[2]*' is a specific subset of process-architecture where the 'how' is hosted on IT.)*

There's nothing complicated about this. There's also almost nothing specific to IT about it; or money either, for that matter. It's always about people, and about structures that help people to achieve aims.

Architectures are not necessarily ❶ *' layered', but intersect as a kind of* ❷ *multi-layered, multi-faceted Venn diagram*

1. Process architecture
Modelling how services connect to deliver a desired outcome, for example the flow through an airport of people and baggage, from end to end.
2. Application architecture
Used to confirm all the computer programs in an organisation work effectively together, for example that 'check-in' can access passport data.

⬠⬠⬠⬠⬠ *Taken from the chapter:* **Enterprise-architecture –**
let's keep it simple

17: Innovation

In uncertain times, innovation is essential.
To help in this, there are plenty of well-known techniques and processes, to guide the creation of new ideas in business. But how well do we support the emotional side of innovation, the real difficulties in expressing new ideas to others, and starting to put them into practice? Sometimes it can take some sidewise thinking to see how the ways in which we respond to incomplete ideas can block the innovation that we need, and what we can do to make it safer for the ideas to flow.

New ideas will always seem irrational at first.
Almost by definition, new ideas are often not *'rational'*. If they don't make sense, it's because to do their job properly they can't make sense: the whole point is that they're moving outside of the known and the certain, which is what's usually meant by *'making sense'*. New ideas move outside of the frame of *'the known'*, in order to create a new frame in which new things can happen; but what we think of as *'rational'* will only work within the confines of the old frame. If we only allow things to work in expected ways, we're limiting our chances for the new.

New ideas move outside of the frame of 'the known'.

Prototypes

A prototype isn't a finished product. A *'beta'* prototype will be usable, but may well have some bugs in. An *'alpha'* prototype should be able to do something useful, but will definitely have gaps and bugs and clunky ideas and probably some awful mistakes too. That's why it's a prototype: to find those mistakes before they get any further. And we usually have to make a lot of mistakes before we get to something that really does work well. Make prototypes a safe space in which to learn from each mistake.

And even an *'alpha'* prototype is quite a long way towards the realising of a new idea. A first prototype may well be no more than a scrawl on the back of a napkin, a crude lash-up made up of paper cups and string. When you're looking at any early-stage work on a new idea, the most important failure to watch out for is a failure of our own imagination.

Scaffolding

New ideas need scaffolding to hold them up. In the early stages, that scaffolding will itself be fragile. If you ridicule new ideas, what you're really saying to others is that you're more interested in playing the playground bully than in helping anything new get going. So again don't complain that nothing much seems to get off the ground when you're around. When ideas are in their first formative stages, that's when they're at their most fragile. And they'll often need your active help to hold them up long enough to get even the first scaffolding in place. And scaffolding isn't pretty. It often looks a mess. And it usually has its own structure, its own way of holding itself together, with little or no connection as such to what it's holding up, in fact much of the scaffolding isn't attached to the final structure at all, but is simply there to provide a means to work on that inner structure.
Trust that it'll be taken down when the time is right, and not before.

Foundations

For a long time, the early stages of implementing any new idea will look like the early stages of a building-site: a great big muddy hole in the ground that's of no use to anyone. But if those foundations are not there, and are not done right, the final structure will fall over. The bigger the new idea, the deeper its foundations will need to go.

And foundations aren't something we can leave out. We can not go back afterwards and put them in later. Foundations take time to build; and they have their own structure, too, which can vary quite a bit from place to place, depending on the ground in which they are set. Every bit as much thought needs to go into the foundations as it does into what goes *'up top'*, even though we will never see those foundations again.

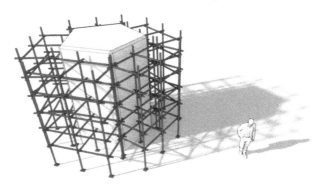

New ideas need scaffolding to hold them up.

⬠⬠⬠⬠⬠ *Taken from the chapter:* **On innovation, foundations,**
scaffolding and Portakabins

18: Back to basics

Here is a simple set of principles that can help to guide all of your sense-making, decision-making, action and review.

1.Things work better when they work together, on purpose

The aim is effectiveness, over the medium to longer-term, not just short-term efficiency, which is still the most common *(and most often destructive)* focus. And we can always do it better, we need to support continuous learning in every context.

2. Any context, any scope, any scale

One key part of getting things to work better, together, on purpose, is that we need to be consistent in how we work across domains, scopes and scales. Unfortunately, that's exactly what does not happen with some current approaches, which are built around domain-specific specialism, with nothing to link all of the different specialisms and perspectives together. To make things work together, we need to ensure that things can work together, tools, methods and more, consistently, across every context, scope and scale.

3. Find the right question

The usual assumption is that what we need most is *'the right answer'*. But in contexts of change, where each *'answer'* is always context-specific and context-dependent, what often matters more is we can find the right question. To quote Eliyahu M.Goldratt:

*"An expert is not someone who gives you the answer,
it is someone who asks you the right question".*

The common experience is that the answers we need will arise all but automatically when we find the right way to frame the question. We need our tools to provide explicit support to *'finding the right question'*. And, especially, to support us in being our own *'expert'*, wherever, as is so often the case in contexts of change, there could be no other expert but ourselves.

4. Work with uncertainty

Every enquiry within a context of change is by its nature, uncertain. When we start out we do not know *(all of)* *'the answer'* that we should arrive at by the end. Often, we're likely to bounce around in uncertainty for quite a while, like a pinball, before any kind of certainty arises at all. We need our tools to work from often-chaotic beginnings to near certain endings, and work consistently and with full connection across all parts of that process.

5. "I don't know… It depends… Just enough…"
This is one that we can visualise as follows:

"I don't know"
We need to be able to say this, in order to face and work with uncertainty, and our tools need to support us in saying this.

"It depends"
Our tools need to be able to help us in exploring dependencies in any type of context, any scope and any scale.

"Just enough"
Our tools need to support us in *'just enough detail'* to enable appropriate decision-making without drowning in *'analysis-paralysis'*.
'Just enough process' to guide exploration without getting in the way.
'Just enough certainty' to enable confidence within action; and many other forms of *'just enough'*.

6. Discipline at all times, even within uncertainty
Another essential *'Just enough…'* concern that all tools must support is *'just enough discipline',* discipline in naming, structures, processes and more. By the nature of the work, the forms of discipline needed will necessarily change the whole time.

7. Each tool or template is a guide to thinking, not a substitute for thinking
Perhaps the single most important point is that no tool does anything on its own. It is an aid to thinking and exploration, and not a substitute for either. Although a tool can and should provide some form of guidance, the questing is always done by the people involved, not by the tool itself. The primary role of a tool is to provide guidance, typically in the form of a visual checklist, to obtain insights, and to provide a structured means to capture insights. It's not merely about making lists, but about gathering insights by moving from place to place in the frame.
Although each could be viewed *(and even used)* as a simple tick the-box checklist, the more usual role of tools such as **Five Elements** is more like a spreadsheet, each thing we add or do may imply changes elsewhere in the spreadsheet, that in turn ripple elsewhere throughout the spreadsheet.

19: What is architecture?

What is architecture? What do we do in architecture? And how do
we do it?
It is essentially the same for every kind of architecture:
enterprise-architecture, solutions-architecture, software-architecture,
building-architecture, naval-architecture, brand-architecture, whatever.

Right down at the root, in principle, architecture is incredibly simple.
It all comes down to just one idea, one aim: *that things work better when
everything works together, on purpose.*

Right down at the root, in practice, architecture is incredibly hard.
It all comes down to just one aim, one requirement: *that everything
works together with everything else, on purpose.*

Efficient; reliable; elegant; integrated; on purpose. That's what
architecture is all about.

Not just for some things, though, but all things, everything, over all of the
scopes and scales and time-scales and content and contexts that might
be required, on time, on budget, and on purpose. And that there is some
kind of shared-purpose around which everything and everyone can work
together, on time, on budget, and on purpose.

What we end up with should be simple, or as simple as possible and
practicable, anyway. But we often have to go through a lot of complexity
before we arrive at that simplicity:
People, processes, politics and petty feuds, technology, temper-tantrums,
structure, story, hopes, fears, wishful-thinking, delusions, disasters, doubts,
debt-collectors, nightmares of logic and logistics, lost-in-translation tangles,
things that just don't work, things that do work in surprising ways, and
maybe a little bit of magic, too: successful architecture covers and copes
with all of that, and more.
So architecture is simple. But it is not easy, in fact it's often just about as far
from easy as it's possible to get.

Things work better when everything works together, on purpose.

⬡⬡⬡⬡⬡ *Taken from the chapter: **Architecture is simple***

20: Vision, role, mission, goal

One of my main frustrations about standard business-strategy frameworks is that they start way too far down, as if the organisation is the centre of the world. The framework I use starts much higher:

Vision: describes a desired *'world'* This is always larger than the organisation, and never *'achieved'.*

Role or roles: what the organisation aims to do and not do within that *'world'.* This identifies where the organisation intersects with customers, partners, stakeholders and so on, this will change slowly over time.

Mission or missions: existing/new capabilities and/or services the organisation intends to create *(via Goals)* and maintain. This is measurable, does not end when *'achieved',* will change with normal business strategy cycle. It is frequently misunderstood or poorly described as *'vision'.*

Goal or goals: project with a specified set of deliverables and a target date for completion. This is not measurable as such, other than conformance with deliverables and/or completion date, should end on completion, will change frequently. Occasionally misunderstood or poorly described as *'vision',* with disastrous results.

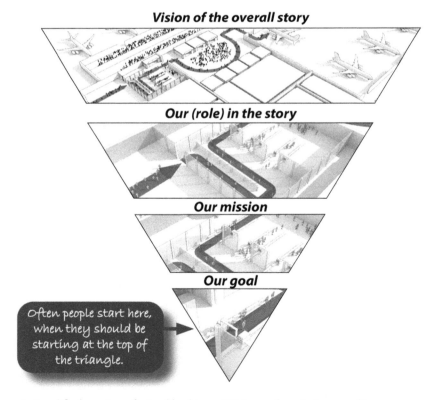

Vision of the overall story

Our (role) in the story

Our mission

Our goal

Often people start here, when they should be starting at the top of the triangle.

A simplified version of a tool looking at Vision, role, mission, goal in use exploring improving the customer journey in an airport.

⬠⬠⬠⬠⬠ *Taken from the chapter:* **Vision, role, mission, goal**

21: Inside and out

Inside-in, inside-out, outside-in, outside-out

How to describe some key distinctions about the way we view our
architecture, about how we see its role, and its relationship with everything
else in its context? There is a simple two-axis matrix we can use for this:
• where we focus, inside *(centred on our own internal context)* or outside *(from
the broader context, where everything is 'the centre', all at the same time)*
• where we look for the business-drivers, in *(looking inward to our own
context)* or out *(looking outward to the broader context)*

This gives us four types of perspectives onto the architecture(s):
• **inside-in** *(How an organisation views itself)*
• **inside-out** *(How an organisation views the enterprise)*
• **outside-in** *(How an enterprise views the organisation, if at all)*
• **outside-out** *(How an enterprise views itself, including possibly
the organisation)*

*A simplified version of the Inside-out tool, the full version can be seen in
the book: '**Tools for Change-mapping**', available online.*

Note that each of these perspectives is valid in its own way. But if we use an inappropriate perspective for a given task, things can go very badly wrong, so we do need to be clear which perspective we're using at any time, and why.

Inside-in is where we focus on a single specific context, and assess it in its own terms. Within this perspective, we assume that the external business-drivers remain the same. It is solely about the internal view, about enhancing internal consistency, internal efficiency and effectiveness. This is the kind of perspective for the *'clean up the mess'* type of architecture-work that must be done to create stable foundations for subsequent strategic development.

Inside-out is where we focus on a single context, and assess the impact of changes in the external business-drivers on that context. This is a perspective that we do need for domain-architectures.

Outside-out is about understanding the broader context in its own terms, regardless of how our own organisation acts within the context; everywhere and nowhere is *'the centre'* of the architecture, all at the same time. In other words, it's about the *'big-picture'* of the *'extended-enterprise'* or *'shared-enterprise'* context.

Outside-in is about understanding our choices in how our own context can play a valued part within the broader shared-enterprise context. Typical examples of views used within this perspective include *customer-journey mapping*[1], *value-network analysis*[2] and *whole-supply-chain modelling*[3]. Note, though, that this perspective is as much about our own organisation's vision, values and policies in relation to those *touchpoints*[4] and *value-flows*[5], as it is to the touch-points, etc themselves. The business-drivers for the overall shared-enterprise are described more within the *'outside-out'* perspective, whereas this is more about that broader context interacts with our concerns and choices.

---

1. **Customer journey mapping**, *modelling what happens from the customer's perspective, how they feel at each step, say at security.*
2. **Value-network analysis**, *how all of the parts connect, how all parts of airport connect to generate and maintain value for customer.*
3. **Whole supply-chain modelling**, *all the elements, including that come from outside, who will maintain the x-ray machines, for example?*
4. **Touch-points** *are areas where your organisation can connect with the customer, for example on a website or where passengers check-in.*
5. **Value-flows**, *in an airport context, this might be the passenger's journey from entering the airport to boarding the plane. At each stage of that journey how value is created and maintained, such as friendly and speedy service through security.*

Implications in EA practice

For viable enterprise-architectures, all of these perspectives will be required: *inside-in, inside-out, outside-out and outside-in.*
A full-scope architecture-development would typically use these perspectives in the following sequence:

- **inside-in**: develop a broad understanding of what clean-up would be required within each domain in scope.
- **outside-out**: develop a broad understanding of the overall business-ecosystem, in its own terms, independent of our own organisation.
- **outside-in**: develop a broad to detailed understanding of how others would interact and transact with our organisation, from their perspective.
- **inside-out** *(usually together with a detailed inside-in)*: develop a detailed architecture for each domain, each from its own perspective, drawing on each of the previous perspectives for guidance.

In practice, there will always be some iteration between these perspectives, and *'inside-in'* and *'outside-out'* can be switched over if preferred. In effect, though, this sequence above defines the precursor-order: an *'outside-in'* perspective will depend on clarity about the overall context, as described by *'outside-out'*; and an *'inside-out'* perspective will only be viable if all of the other views are already in place.

A narrow-scope domain-architecture development will often need to use only an *'inside-out'* and/or *'inside-in'* perspective. *(This applies to all domain-architectures: IT, business-of-the-business, HR, environment, security, safety and so on.)* This will be valid if the broad-context work has already been done and is available to guide the selection of relevant *'external'* business-drivers. If the broad context work has not been done, a narrow-scope development is almost guaranteed to cause architecture-fragmentation problems.

Very few current architecture-frameworks cover the full set of perspectives. Some current mainstream *'enterprise'*-architecture frameworks are actually domain-architectures, typically focussed primarily or exclusively on IT, and incorporating only either *'inside-in'* and/or *'inside-out'* perspectives. They can and usually do work well as guides for domain-architectures; but without the ability to create or use *'outside-out'* and/or *'outside-in'* views, they are all but guaranteed to be problematic if attempts are made to use those frameworks for true whole-of-enterprise architectures.

⬡⬡⬡⬡⬡ *Taken from the chapter:* **Inside-in, inside-out, outside-in, outside-out**

22: Capability

Defining capability

Capability:
the ability to do something.

Capability-based planning:
planning to do something, based on capabilities that already exist, and/or that will be added to the existing suite of capabilities; also, identifying the capabilities that would be needed to implement and execute a plan.

Capability increment:
an extension to an existing capability; also, a plan to extend a capability.

Capability map: a visual and/or text description of an organisation's capabilities.

Note what else is intentionally not in that definition of *'capability'*:

• there's no actual doing, it's just an ability to do something, not the usage of that ability.
• there's no *'how'*, we don't assume anything about how that capability works, or what it's made up of.
• there's no *'why'*, we don't assume any particular purpose.
• there's no *'who'*, we don't assume anything about who's responsible for this capability, or where it sits in an organisational hierarchy or suchlike.

We do need all of those items, of course, as we start to flesh out the details of how the capabilities would be implemented and used in real-world practice. But in the core-definition itself, we very carefully don't, they must not be included in the definition itself.

The reason why we have to be so careful about this is because the relationship between service, capability and function is that each of them contains all of the others, which in turn each contain all of the others, and so on almost to infinity. If we don't use deliberately-generic definitions for all of those items, we get ourselves into a tangle very quickly indeed.

In principle there are many different ways in which we could sort out the relationships between definitions, but the one I've found simplest in practice, and the one I often use in modelling, is to start from a statement that everything is a service. This then gives us a set of relationships between assets, capabilities, functions and various other types of items contained *'within'* each service, that we could represent visually as follows on the next page.

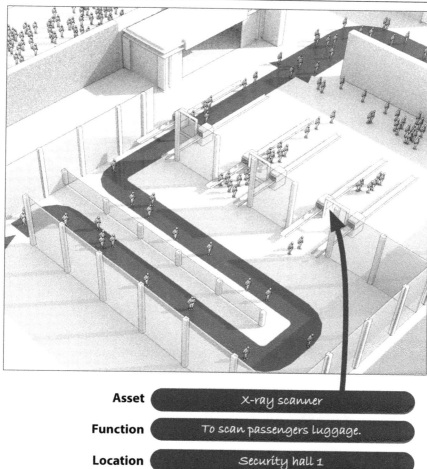

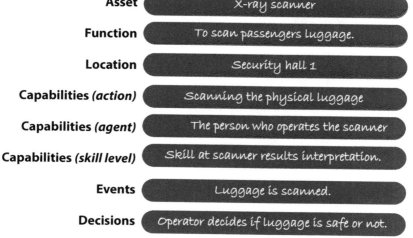

Asset	X-ray scanner
Function	To scan passengers luggage.
Location	Security hall 1
Capabilities *(action)*	Scanning the physical luggage
Capabilities *(agent)*	The person who operates the scanner
Capabilities *(skill level)*	Skill at scanner results interpretation.
Events	Luggage is scanned.
Decisions	Operator decides if luggage is safe or not.

A simplified capability map for an airport security check area.
Note that in this example only one asset (the x-ray scanner) has been shown.
Each asset is made up a mix of four types of value: Physical, Virtual, Relational
and Aspirational. (These value types are described in the
Tools for Change-mapping book, available online).

Note that *'capability'* in the above diagram is split into three subcomponents:
- **action**: what kind of 'thing' *(or combinations of 'things')* that the capability can act on.
- **agent**: what kind of *'thing'* does the *'doing'* in the capability.
- **skill-level**: in essence, the level of variation and uncertainty that the agent(s) and the overall capability can handle

Again, remember that all capabilities are made up of services that are made up of all of the above, that in turn are made up of services that are made up of services, which are made up of services and ,so on

Another theme that I've explored is how capability, function and service actually fit together. For example:
- everything in the enterprise is or represents or signifies a service.
- a process links services together in some way to achieve some kind of outcome
- a function is an external view of a service - in effect, a description of its interfaces *('black-box' view)*, often together with a summary or overview of what it does and how it does it *('white-box' view)*
- a capability is the ability to do something
- a function needs to be linked to a capability in order to do anything
- on its own, a capability literally has no function
- in a service-architecture, we link together a function and a capability *(and various other service-content items, as in the diagram above)* in order to create a service

A simple worked example of security check in an airport[1]:
- *everything in the enterprise is or represents or signifies a service.*

Enterprise of security check.

Get people and luggage
checked and out.

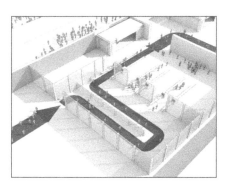

Example continued overleaf.

---

1. *Perspective. This simple example is viewing only its own part of the overall enterprise, so this would be like **'Inside-In'** as described in the last chapter. While focusing on what just the baggage department makes sense, it should always be in the context of the overall enterprise: **'Outside-out'**. Otherwise a solution which would suit the baggage department could be at the expense of the overall enterprise.*

Enterprise of security check: *Process*

1. Move passengers from check-in

2. Slow down line of passengers to avoid bottlenecks

3. Scan luggage and passengers

4. Move passengers out of area

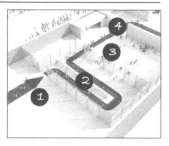

Enterprise of security check: *Service*
(A service is typically made up of these parts:)

1. Asset (such as an x-ray scanner)

2. Function (what asset does, eg scans)

3. Location (where asset is)

4. Capability-A (job to be done, eg scan bags)

4. Capability-B (agent, eg the x-ray scanner)

4. Capability-C (skill, eg x-ray sensitivity)

5. Event (eg passenger arrives in our area)

6. Decision (eg have bags passed all checks)

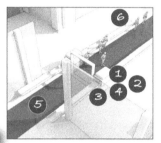

23: Fractals and EA

One of the huge challenges of trying to make things simple in a complex context is that often it can make things seem more complicated. For a while, anyway, until things settle down a bit, and the reasoning behind the simplification starts to become more clear.

A main focus for me has been around developing methods and frameworks for the kind of deeply-fractal[1], complex contexts that we're facing more and more in whole-enterprise architectures.
By cross-linking and cross-comparing between many different methods and metaphors I created a method that's both simple enough and fractal enough to be usable for any scope, any scale, any type of context, any type of content, and still remain essentially consistent everywhere across that range. We could summarise that method visually as described in Chapter 6. Overleaf we see this method used to ask a set of questions in an airport issue, in a simple tool-sheet.

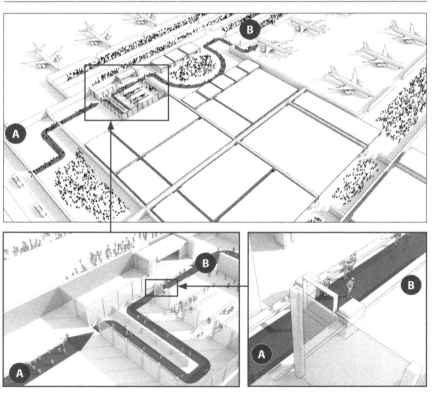

1. Fractals, in brief, are patterns which are similar at any scale. This principle can used to explain Whole EA , for example an airport. In this simple example an airport is trying to is get people from A to B, in any or all areas.

⬠⬠⬠⬠⬠ *Taken from the chapter: **What What? and other taxonomic tangles***

24: How to use the Five Elements

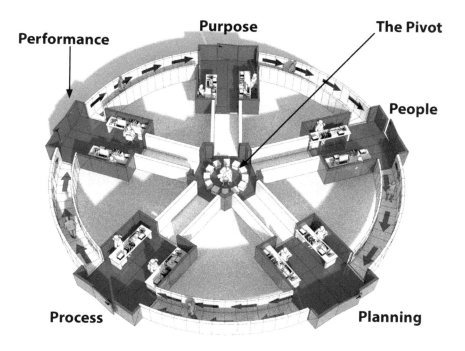

A simplified version of the Five Elements tool used to explore the issue of improving airport security.

Using the Five Elements to explore an issue
As mentioned earlier I designed the **Five Elements** as simple tool to ask questions. As it is designed to work for *any* context, it can't reasonably have *every* question or *every* answer. But what it does do is to get conversations started, get questions being asked, using a simple order.
The problem is that it's actually quite hard to demonstrate something that can do anything, so here we will pick one example to show how it works.

Improving airport security
Having a real world example can help clarify how the **Five Elements** works, so if we imagine that a change department in an airport have been tasked with improving airport security. They would start in the *'Purpose'* room and ask these types of questions. We have supplied some *typical* answers, to show the *kind* of things you would be looking for.

Purpose / Why:
• What's going on here?
"We have been tasked with improving airport security. (We are the change department in an international airport)."
Continued overleaf.

• What's the question?

"There are quite a few questions including, why is this important? What happens if it is not resolved? We will answer why does airport security need changing first, before rushing to change it, potentially in the wrong way."

• Who's asking, and why are they asking?

"The board have tasked us with this as there has been a lot of complaints from the media and the public."

• Who's paying for this?

"The airport is part owned by shareholders and the local government, so the budget would be funded partly by private and public funds."

• Who's really paying for this?

"The 'this' is important. Paying to explore the issue of improving airport security, is quite different to paying to actually improving airport security. Paying to explore the issue, we would say the board."

• What's the real question here, their real 'Why'?

"Why does the board feel the issue is worth exploring or resolving? Why is it important? What benefits and to who, will exist if things are improved? What does 'improved' mean?"

• How do we find out what the real question is?

"We feel before we start changing anything, we need to know what's going on now. Once we know that we can see how, if anything can be improved. So we will explore the state of airport security first."

• What are the real vision, values and principles that must apply here?

"The board has some kind of vision of what 'improved airport security' is. So we need to know what that is and what is valued by them and other stakeholders, so that any solution satisfies all stakeholders".

• When and where is **this**[1] about?

"The 'when' of exploring the issue, we estimate 2 months, the 'when' of actually improving airport security', we again estimate maybe 2 months".

• Where should this be done, and by whom?

"One of the main areas is actually in the airport security area of the airport, to observe, what is going on. And interview front-line staff."

• Why should it be done by those people, and not someone else?

"We need people who are actually doing airport security, to understand, why things are done in the way they are, and what they feel could be improved".

Continued overleaf.

---

1. Which 'this'?

Deciding which **'this'** we are actually talking about can get very confusing. In our airport example, do we mean **'this'**:

is 'A' exploring the issue of how to improve baggage handling.

or

'B' actually improving baggage handling?

It might seem that it is 'B', as we want to improve baggage handling, but this could be disastrous if we have not explored it first. We might initiate a 'better' baggage handling system, but if we don't know how it works currently, we could unleash mayhem. So in this example we can assume that the people involved have yet to explore, let alone change the baggage handling system.

• When does the requester need an answer?

"Ideally before the summer season, as if changes are deemed necessary, then we should make those changes in a quiet period."

• How will we know when we have a useful and usable answer?

"When we have a clear understanding of what is going on now, and what could happen if things went wrong."

• What are the criteria for a useful answer?

"A clear picture of whether to change how things are done now. And what people are aiming for in the future, and if that is actually feasible."

One of the main points of the '**Purpose**' room is understand the *'Why'* of an issue. *What is actually going on? Do we actually want to change anything?* In our simple example the change department is assuming nothing and want to find out what is going on now, before changing anything.

After the *'**Purpose**'* room we will move to the *'**People**'* room and answer the following types of questions:

People/Who:
• Who's involved in this?

"We can use the Whole EA tool as described in previous chapters to map out all the stakeholders, such as passengers, government regulators and so on".

• What kind of stake are they holding?

"We can use the Value tool[1] to assess, what value each stakeholder obtains from their stake in the enterprise."

• What kind of sharp-pointed stake can they point at us…?

"We need to understand what fines and punishments could be faced if this was to go wrong, such as getting fired, but not that we are crippled by fear to rush for the easiest answer."

• What are their drivers, their own *'Why'* in each case?

"It would be useful to do a 'customer' journey, for each stakeholder to better understand what is important to them and why."

---

1. *The Value tool. This tool is fully described in the **Tools for Change-mapping** book, but in brief everything has at least four types of value. Much more than just money, which can affect people's stake in something. For example, while a passenger may seem to value money above anything, (part of virtual), their own and their loved ones safety is of far higher value. Working around the boxes leads to new insights.*

Virtual	Relational
Passenger does not want to waste money in the airport.	Passenger's family who are travelling with them.
Physical	Aspirational
My safety and loved ones is of the up-most value.	I want to feel that the airport cares about me and who travels with us

• What kind of power-issues are there within this?

"We need to understand what power means to each stakeholder, which seems linked to what each stakeholder values. For example if front line staff feel able to do their jobs effectively, if the board uses AI to replace people, if they complain about working conditions."

• Who's avoiding what, and why?

"What are the responsibilities (RACI)[1] of each stakeholder. Why do they not want to do a task? Is it deemed out of their role? If they do it will anyone even notice?"

• Who's dumping what, on whom, and why?

"Again RACI should help us understand what is happening, such as say the Change department may just tell the security department to sort the issue, without saying how to sort the issue. Also SEMPER[2] can help."

• What will make each of the stakeholders happy?

"The SEMPER tool and the Value tool can show what people want, such as they can make suggestions in the workplace and are listened to."

• Who can we engage in this, how, and why?

"The Whole EA tool can show who. As a guess we need to engage all stakeholders so they feel part of security improvements, rather than it's just been dumped on them from 'on-high'."

• Who can we not engage in this, how, and why?

"Certain security details have to remain restricted for obvious reasons from certain people such as passengers."

• How can we make this easier, for everyone?

"Clear communication, proper planning and testing. Working out who is doing what and when. Planning for proper transition"

• What are the rules, regulations, policies, guidelines, principles here?

"The stakeholders should be able to give us the exact rules, regulations, etc. And possibly by asking other airports."

• Who decides on each of those rules, and why?

"Again the stakeholders should be able to tell us this, as at this time we are unsure, without more information."

The '***People***' room has given us an idea of who is or could be involved with our issue, such as improving airport security. Typically we would then move on to the '***Planning***' room. Remembering that in this example we are not planning the '*improved security*', rather planning how to explore the issue of '*how to improve airport security*'. As said before, if we just go straight to planning 'improvements' without fully understanding the situation now, all kinds of mayhem could ensue.

---

1. RACI tool
Looks at who is Responsible, Accountable, Consulted and Informed within an issue. There seems some disagreement online who invented it back in the 1950s.
2. SEMPER
*A tool designed to act as a questionnaire to assess what is happening within an organisation. It is fully described in the **Tools for Change-mapping** book. Each question has a score out of five, with different scores highlighting different issues, such as a lack of motivation.*

Planning/How:

Here we will plan how to explore the issue of airport security, and on another iteration of the Five Elements, we would use this same room to plan the improvements *(if the exploration had shown that changing things was in the best interest of all stakeholders).*

• What are we going to do?

"We are going to observe how airport security works now, for all stakeholders."

• How are we going to do it?

"Have a team observe and interview stakeholders for 3 weeks at all times and then present that information to the change-team."

• What framework or method fits best for what, and why?

"We need to look into this, but not take too long debating about which method. Maybe it's better to just get started and adapt our approach to fit the situation, rather than the other way around."

• When should we use each method, in what sequence?

"Again the stakeholders should be able to tell us this, as at this time we are unsure, without more information."

• Where should we apply each method, and with whom, for whom?

"For now, we will observe and then interview, a bit like an after action review, and see how that works."

• What resources do we need to make this happen, where, and when?

"Having a team observing at all hours for 3 weeks will need setting up in itself[1]."

• What kind of plan do we need for each stage of the action?

"We could work backwards. If we know what the intended end date is and then see if it's possible to do in the allotted time."

• How do we plan for how to change the plan, where, when and why?

"If we run the plan for a week and if it needs improving, adjust it then."

• What information do we need to capture as we go along?

"In part, how the process of security works, timings, problem areas, what front-line staff views are. But we also need to record our own process of observing and interviewing, so that we can improve our own techniques."

• When do we start, what's the trigger for when we start?

"We will start next week and review how the observations are proceeding after one week. The whole exploration will be within 2 months."

• When do we stop, what's the signal to stop?

"When we feel we have enough to decide if to change how airport security is done or not."

---

1. *Sometimes unknowns will need to be solved before the main issue can be explored or resolved. This is where the fractal nature of things can cause problems. You can use the Five Elements 'in miniature' to explore the smaller issue (such as setting up observers, for 3 weeks), which will then help the main issue (exploring airport security) proceed.*

As we can see, by this stage things can start to get very complicated very quickly. The **Five Elements** acts as a set of questions, but if you find that keeping track of what bit you are doing is getting a bit confusing a more mechanical version of the **Five Elements** called **Change-mapping** can help.

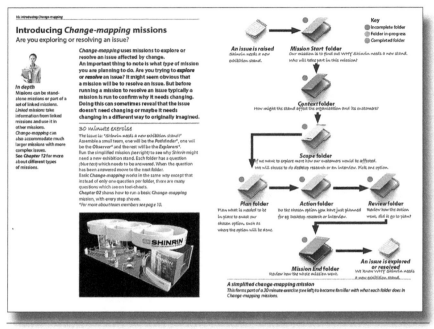

*A sample page from the first (of three) **Change-mapping** books.*

Process/What:

This 'room' or stage is where the plan is enacted. The questions here act as guidance in the middle of action. For example if the team are observing a security department and they are so busy watching what's happening, they forget to actually write anything down! Often the best plan will fail when meeting the real world, so they need to know when to stick to the plan or abandon the plan.

To continue our worked example we can imagine at this stage one of the teams are observing airport security during a busy afternoon and when they have a spare minute write down some of the answers to these questions:

• What's happening right now, with whom, where, when?

"We are recording the movement of passengers moving through the secure area in the early morning rush."

• What information and ideas are we capturing as we go along?

"We have noticed that the passengers are slowed down by staff members, at certain points to avoid jams at the hand luggage check area."

Continued overleaf.

• How and where do we store any information and ideas that we capture?

"We had planned to video the secure area, but we were told that this was not possible for various reasons, so we are taking written notes."

• How do we switch between methods and frameworks, in the midst of the action?

"To be honest when everything is happening at once, it's mostly just a mad rush to write down what's happening."

• Who's responding, how, where, when and why, to what?

"We tend to rotate each hour as it can be exhausting noting down every detail and it can become repetitive. Also we found that we were actually getting in the way, which was not popular."

• What do all those rules, guidelines, principles, values and so on mean here in practice?

"We are trying, but we have found that the plan didn't know about small details, which tend to knock everything else out of alignment. But there was no way of knowing, without just having a go."

• How are we managing the Architect's Mantra of *'I don't know', 'It depends'* and *'Just enough detail'*?

"We have used this a lot as we found sticking rigidly to the plan at first was not working."

• How do we know when to keep going, and why?

"Despite a few cross words from staff and passengers, we kept going all by keeping out the way, which actually meant people were acting more as they would typically."

• How do we know when to stop?

"As mentioned before, tiredness, was an unexpected factor, which impacted on quality, so we take regular breaks. For the overall exercise, after 3 weeks we found that no new information seemed to be appearing so we stopped."

Performance/Outcome:

Of course there can be multiple enactments and plans, but for simplicty we are just looking at what happened after the team were in the secure area, rather than at the end of the entire observation of airport security.
These types of questions would be asked:

• What was supposed to happen?

"We were meant to record security checks for 3 weeks as part of a 2 month exploration of airport security."

• What actually happened?

"We found that by 3 weeks no new information was being revealed so stopped there."

• What was the source of the difference, and why?

"We had not known about patterns of work, which were repeated almost always during the 3 week period."

Continued overleaf.

• What did we learn from this?

"We had to quickly adapt to a new method of recording the security checks, as our chosen method of video recording was not appropriate."

• How did that answer the initial question?

"The change team needed to know how airport security was working now, and we felt that we have answered that question. We provided a written report highlighting our finds."

• What was the value that we gained from exploring the question?

"The change team can now base their recommended changes to airport security on actual evidence, rather than assumptions."

• What needs to change, for whom and by whom, to do it better next time?

"If were to repeat this exercise, keeping out of the way, would be the main thing and solving the video problem as well."

• What commitments do we each need to make, to make that happen?

"Telling people the benefits of video recording and ensuring those recordings are kept securely, would be very useful."

• What new questions do these answers raise, why, and for whom?

"Are there better ways to observe lots of action at once, more people, more cameras?."

Of course there would be lots more 'Who', 'What', 'When', 'Why', 'Where', 'How', questions there, as anyone who's worked in the field for any length of time would know all too well.

A method is a work-instruction that is hard-wired to a single context, and can only be used reliably within that single context.
A *metamethod* is a procedure from which context-specific methods can be derived. Although each individual derived-method may cover only a narrow scope, the total scope that can be covered by the set of derived-methods is limited only by any built-in constraints of the *metamethod*.

The trade-off, is that a method looks easier to use, because everything's already provided for us; whereas a *metamethod* always requires us to be much more careful about assumptions. And to think carefully about scope and scale and boundaries and so on. But the latter are very necessary things to do when we don't or can't know beforehand what the scope or scale or context-boundaries would be.

In the *metamethod* here, we use our experience to choose which methods and frameworks are appropriate to the needs of the context, and swap them in and out as the needs of the work would require.
Doing it this way round might seem more complicated at the start, but once we get used to it, and how it works in practice, this really is a whole lot simpler. And the added advantage is that we really can work with any scope, any scale, any content, any context. We do have be more careful, to apply a lot more rigour, be more explicit about assumptions and so on.

⬠⬠⬠⬠⬠ *Taken from the chapter: **What What? and other taxonomic tangles***

25: The relationship is the asset

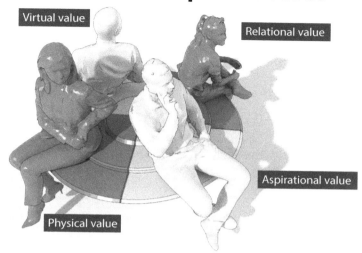

Value can be made up of four parts, which must be in balance. In brief they are: Virtual (information, etc), Relational (connections between people), Physical (size, weight, etc) and Aspirational (what it means to someone)

"Our people are our greatest asset!"

How often have you heard that phrase? How often have you used that phrase yourself? But how often have you stopped to think about what it means? And what it implies in real business practice?

No doubt it's intended as a compliment, a statement of collective pride and purpose. Yet this well-meant platitude can conceal a fundamental flaw in business reasoning, a flaw so serious that it can easily destroy an entire enterprise. The key is that it all depends on what we mean by *'asset',* which in turn depends on what we mean by *'ownership'*.

An asset is an item of value that is owned. Yet there are two fundamentally different concepts of ownership: possession, and responsibility. In most common usage, especially in business, it's the former meaning that applies: to *'own'* something is to possess it; *"possession is nine-tenths of the law"*, and suchlike expressions.

Which is a problem. If *'our'* implies possession, and we then say *"Our people are our greatest asset"*, it becomes all too easy to view people as assets that we possess. Objects, or subjects, perhaps, that we have an inherent, inalienable right to exploit in any way we need, just as with any other asset.

The only time that people are *'assets'* is when they are slaves. So to describe people as *'assets'* is not a compliment: it's more like an insult, an overt declaration of intent to enslave.

Not exactly a wise move in present-day business, especially if we need the continued commitment, collaboration and cooperation of those people in the collective enterprise.
People are not assets.

Yet there is a real asset there; and it's one that does need our active promotion and protection, just as with any other business asset. To get there, though, we need to think differently.

First, drop the idea that ownership equates to possession: in this context at least, it doesn't, and it can't. The only kind of ownership that works here is responsibility-based: to *'own'* something is to acknowledge and act on one's personal responsibilities to, toward and for that *'something'*.

Next, we move back up one step. The person is not the asset: it is the relationship with that person that is the asset.

The relationship is the asset.

Or rather, there are two distinct forms of relationship here that are *'the asset'*: the links between people and the collective, the enterprise, the corporation, business-unit, department, work-team, and the links between individuals. One illustration of this distinction is the phrase *"people join companies and leave people"*: they create a relationship that is an asset they share with the company, but leave because person-to-person relationships with others in the company, an overly-demanding manager, for example, have changed from positive-value assets to negative-value liabilities.

These assets are fundamentally different from physical assets *(conventional 'property')* and virtual assets *('intellectual property')*. Not only can they never be *'possessed'* as such, but they actually exist only as responsibilities, in the sense of *'response-ability'*. In both cases, they're strongly dependent on feelings, probably far more so than anything concrete, in fact.
The relationship with the collective is an odd kind of *'one-way'* link from the person to the company or whatever, which depends on abstract feelings about reputation and *'belonging'* and the like; there is nothing that we within the company can do directly to change that *(though a great deal that we can do indirectly to change it, especially if we're not aware of the relational impact of what we do and don't do)*. The person-to-person link is more direct, often literally visceral, and importantly depends on the responsibility of both parties to maintain it: if either party drops their end of the relationship, the link is lost.

People only become *'our'* people when those relationships exist: abstract links with the shared enterprise, and personal links with the other people in the enterprise with whom they interact. The connection with the enterprise, and so the ability to engage in and contribute to the enterprise, depends almost entirely on the strength of those relationships.

Physical presence may mean almost nothing: *'presenteeism[1]'* is endemic in most large organisations.

It's only when people are emotionally present that things start to happen: and they can only be emotionally present if the relationships exist to enable them to do so.

The relationship is exactly like any other business asset:

• how do you measure the value of the asset?
• how do you convert a liability *(negative-value)* to an asset *(positive-value)*, and prevent an asset from becoming a liability?
• how do you monitor depreciation, wear, and other forms of erosion of value of the asset?
• how do you maintain the asset itself, in order to maintain the value of the asset?

You already do much of this in a sales-development process, from prospect to contact to pre-sales to sales-point to after-sales to maintenance and follow-up. A continuing sales-relationship is a high-value asset, as long as it remains of value to both parties. That last point is where many so-called *'customer-relationship management'* systems will fail: they only check the value from the company's perspective, not the clients', and so pester *'high value'* clients to the extent that the latter will drop the relationship from their end, a fact that will not, however, be noticed by the system, because it has no means to do so. Note though, that this only works if we take a responsibility-based approach to the asset: the moment we think that we *'possess'* the customer is where it all starts to go horribly wrong…

The same is true for employee-relationships. People are not assets: the assets are the relationships through which employees feel themselves to belong as *'our people'*. To be *'our'*, to be a member of *'us'*, is a relationship with and as one of *'us'.* The relationship is the asset through which we connect with *'our people'*, through which employees are 'our people'.

So how do you measure that asset? How do you measure its value? Because if you don't measure the value, from both directions, you have no means to identify when that asset is at risk of becoming a liability.

How do you monitor changes in that value? How do you monitor potential and actual depreciation and wear? What actions do you take to maintain the asset, and the value of that asset? Much as for virtual-assets, how are these relational assets created, reviewed, updated, destroyed? And why and for what purpose would you do each of these actions?

And there are other, more subtle issues around those two different types of relational assets: person-to-person, versus person-to-collective.

---

1. Presenteeism

Working while sick despite having reduced productivity levels or negative consequences. Wikipedia

The purpose of a brand, for example, is to provide an anchor for the latter type of asset: without the brand, or some other means to identify *(and identify with)* the collective, the only relationships that people can have with a company or other collective will be person-to-person. A key concern of personal-service firms, for example, is to link customer-relationships with the company rather than with the person providing the service. Otherwise if and when that person moves on, the company's nominal relationships with clients will move with the person, rather than remain with the company.

In a similar way, if a manager or co-worker damages or destroys a person-to-person relationship with an employee, such as through bullying, for example, the employee will probably move on. But whilst the person-to-person connection then ceases to exist, the company is left with an active liability in terms of damage to reputation and other aspects of that person's relational link with the collective. Which may well fester and infect others' relationships with the company if nothing is done to repair the damage. The opposite is true, too: good reputation extends itself, virally, automatically helping to create high-value relational-assets without additional direct effort by the company and its representatives.

Relationships are assets; relationships matter.

So we need to make a habit, perhaps, to view relationships as assets, in exactly the same way as any other asset. Employees, customers, shareholders, everyone else: no person is an asset. Ever. But every relationship with those people is an asset. And if we fail to take care of that asset, it risks becoming a liability that can drag us down, just as with every other type of asset. The asset is the relationship, and, as an asset, it's always our responsibility to maintain it.

People are not assets: it is the relationship with each person that is the asset.

The asset is the relationship – not the person.

⬠⬠⬠⬠⬠ *Taken from the chapter: **The relationship is the asset***

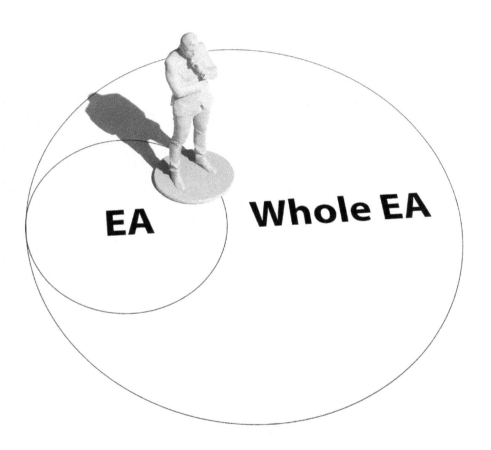

EA

Whole EA

Part 3:

Why Whole Enterprise Architecture?

This section of the book is an abridged version of
'Why Whole Enterprise Architecture?'
www.leanpub.com/tp-whywholeea

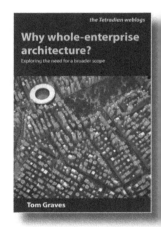

26: Financial-architecture and EA

"There's no way we can do it",
he said with a sigh. *"We can't make the business-case work: there's no way round that great hole in the company accounts."*

It had seemed like a straightforward EA task: discover, determine and decommission outdated and redundant IT-systems, and save wasted money on unused licence-fees and so on.
We had been given the funds to find out what was really going on in the organisation's IT-estate, and so what we could safely remove.
For the next stage, though, we were told we would need to build a *'proper business-case'*: we'd need to be able to prove that what we would save by switching things off would be significantly more than the cost of doing it. And that was where things came unstuck…

In fact, the business-case was obvious, or at least, obvious to anyone who had actually looked at what we had done. The potential savings in licence-fees alone ran into many millions of dollars a year, let alone the more subtle savings from re-using idle servers or freeing-up unneeded real-estate. By comparison, the costs were tiny: in some cases not much more than a few hours of paperwork, and overall perhaps a few staff for a few months at most.

But the sting in the tail was that requirement for proof, in terms of the organisation's standard company-accounts. What we discovered, to our horror, was that the accounts themselves prevented us from doing so: the way those accounts were structured actually made it impossible to make almost any business-case at all for ever shutting anything down. For the whole IT-estate, in essence the accounts-structure was this:

• six large systems listed as line-items, at tens to hundreds of millions of dollars each
• one line-item, labelled *'Other'*, for everything else, as an total of several hundred million dollars

That was it: no detailed-breakdown, no more detail, just that one line-item of *'Other'*. Our work had shown that there was not much we could do with the big-six systems, the ones that had warranted their own line-item each.

(Actually, there was, but we weren't willing to risk it until we'd built enough trust on the smaller change-projects to get the executive to let us do it.) All of the savings that we'd identified and advised were in amongst the hundreds of *'smaller'* applications and systems under the *'Other'* category.

It took us a while to realise the extent to which we were trapped. Whatever we did, the costs of doing the work would show up in the accounts: every change-project had its own private line-item.

But because there was no detailed breakdown for those *'smaller'* systems, all of the savings would vanish into that all-consuming *'Other'.* The result: whichever way we framed it, we always ended up with what looked like a negative business-case, visible costs, invisible savings.

We had no way forward: no proof, so no further project.

But the fact is that it wasn't just us: the company was in a mess. It had blocked itself out of not just from one-off savings of many millions of dollars, but also from savings of millions of dollars every year from foregone software-licence and system-maintenance fees. That was almost a decade ago now, yet as far as I know, they're still paying out those millions every year, for software and systems they don't use, and some cases don't even have any more.

The financial-architecture was unable to support the enterprise-architecture.

Our whole change-project reported to a junior IT-executive who reported to someone else who eventually reported to the CIO, in other words, way too far down the pecking-order for the actual need. To get the necessary changes to happen to either the organisation's business-case processes or, preferably, the accounts-structures as well, we would have had to have the attention of the entire executive board, which is the level at which enterprise-architecture actually belongs, and why it belongs there, too.

Instead, we had the whole board complaining, from a far-off distance, that everything cost too much to run, and we should cut costs wherever we could. And then actively prevented us from doing just that, via poor of financial-architecture design and implementation.

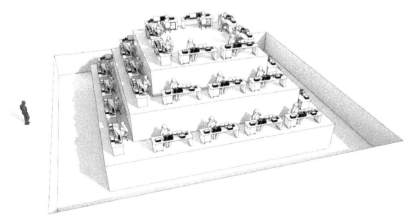

Rigid organisational hierarchies can mean that the people who can make real change, often can't get to the people who can authorise said change.

That wasn't just a one-off, by the way: once we break our enterprise-architectures out of the IT-centric box, these financial-architecture problems can be seen popping up all over the place.

Another example is actually a naming-problem, with rather strong echoes of the problems that arise from the mis-labelling of qualitative requirements as *'non-functional'*, creating the illusion that those requirements don't really have any function, and therefore don't matter. In this case, it's the partitioning of business-units into profit-centres and cost-centres, creating a similar illusion that cost-centres don't contribute in any way to business profits, and therefore should be considered as prime targets for any cost-cutting exercise.

The distinction between *'profit-centre'* and *'cost-centre'* only appears in and as a result of *linear-thinking*. The only difference between them is that a profit-centre has a direct connection to business-revenues *(and business-profit)*, while a *'cost-centre'* has only an indirect connection to revenue. To *linear-thinking*, indirect-connections are all-but-invisible, so much so that they are often said to not even exist.

Yet the moment we use systems-thinking approaches, a whole-of-system view, then that distinction all but disappears.

So whenever enterprise-architecture needs to be involved in any cost-cutting exercise, we need to beware of badly designed financial-architectures, and instead remember to review costs from a systemic perspective, not simply in terms of linear distance from revenue-streams.

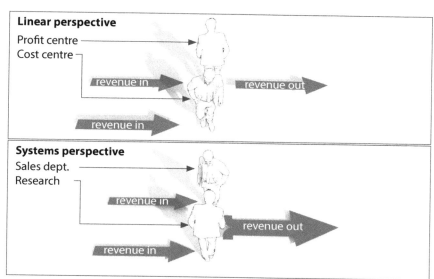

Reviewing costs in a linear way is less effective than a systems view.

⬠⬠⬠⬠⬠ Taken from the chapter: **Financial-architecture and enterprise-architecture**

27: Digital transformation

What is digital transformation?

We can say is that it's about some kind of transformation, probably in some kind of business-context, that involves something that some people call *'digital'*. To put it another way, it is another instance of what happens when a kind of new technology opens up new opportunities to do some aspects of a story, often a business-story, in a new and different way.

Which is a great idea. Usually. At the start, anyway. But there are at least four ways to get it badly wrong:

- We get over-excited about the technology, forgetting that a business-story is always, first and foremost, about people.
- We try to make it benefit only some players, at the expense of others, forgetting that a business-story only works as a whole.
- We fall for the delusion that the technology can do everything, which it can not.
- We hope that the technology will at last give us control over everything.

And unfortunately, any or all of those are exactly what happen, all too often... To illustrate this, let's take a simple model of the relationship between the organisation and the broader shared-enterprise, enterprise as *'bold endeavour'* or shared-story - within which it operates: Using the **Inside Out** model described earlier in Chapter 21.

A simplified version of the Inside-out tool, described in chapter 21.

At the ***inside-in*** level, probably the classic early example of *'digital transformation'* was *business-process reengineering*. It was a great idea: use new technology to take over the tedium of back-office work, and free people up to do more of the work that machines could not do. And there were ways to do it right. But for most, it went wrong, very quickly:

• It was hugely over-hyped by IT-system vendors and the big-consultancies.
• It was sold as an easy way to cut costs, particularly employee costs.
• It was hyped as being able to do all of the work, via predefined *'executable business processes'*.
• It was sold as the way to control everything in the back-office, to force everything to conform to simple lists of *'business rules'.*

Otherwise known, in the real world, as a guaranteed way to mess things up. IT-vendors and big-consultancies made a fortune, of course: but for almost everyone else, it was a hugely expensive mistake, and one from which some organisations never recovered.
Not to mention all the careers and lives ruined in the midst of *'cost-cutting'* in which so many of those organisations had taken part...
The crucial point was that the focus should never have been on the technology alone, instead, much more on the actual tasks to be done, as a whole; and even more, on the people, and the overall people-story. And yet, in most cases, that last point was ignored or glossed over at the time.

A decade later, we saw exactly the same happening again, this time at the ***inside-out*** level, with the rise of web-technologies. It was a great idea: use new technology, together with those business-process technologies, to help organisations open up a new kind of conversation with the wider world. And there were ways to do it right. But for most, it went wrong, very quickly:

• It was hugely over-hyped by IT-system vendors and the big consultancies.
• It was sold as an easy way to sell new products to new markets.
• It was hyped as being able to do all of the work, *"build it and they will come"*.
• It was sold as the way to control the market.

Otherwise known, in the real world, as a guaranteed way to mess things up. IT-vendors and big-consultancies made a fortune, of course: but for almost everyone else, it was a hugely expensive mistake, and one from which some organisations never recovered. Not to mention angering entire markets in the process...
The crucial point was that the focus should never have been on the technology alone, instead, much more on the actual tasks to be done, as a whole; and even more, on the people, and the overall people-story.

And again, a decade or so later, we're seeing exactly the same happening again, this time at the **outside-in** level, with the rise of so-called digital-transformation. It's a great idea: use new technology, together with those web-technologies and business-process technologies, to enable citizens, customers and others to build their own conversations with the organisation. And there are ways to do it right, which include:

- We need to mitigate against the hype about the technology itself, perhaps particularly from the IT-vendors and big consultancies...
- We need to acknowledge *Conway's Law*[1], and recognise that for digital-transformation to succeed, we need to change the way the organisation communicates with itself.
- We need to be aware that not everything can be done by IT, and design parallel processes accordingly.
- We need to acknowledge that, whatever technology we use, it's always more complex than it looks, and that we need to keep people, not technology, at the centre of every would-be *'solution'*.

Yes, in each case, the technology is important, as an enabler: the new options probably wouldn't exist without that new technology. Yet it's also not about the technology itself, and that point is crucially important. Instead, so-called *'digital transformation'* succeeds only when it's mostly about people and their needs. We forget that fact at our peril.

Conway's Law
States that an organisation's IT system will mirror its organisational setup. Often as an organisation evolves 'quick fixes' become infrastructure rather than more elegant solutions. For example, a hundred years ago airports in the US were small scale fields, who with infrastructure guidance from the US Postal Service eventually became today's airline industry. Many of the reasons for the airline infrastructure are long forgotten, and were likely never designed for such a volume of passengers. How many passengers might be flying in one hundred years time?

⬠⬠⬠⬠⬠ *Taken from the chapter:* **Digital-transformation -it's about (much) more than just digital**

28: Anti-clients

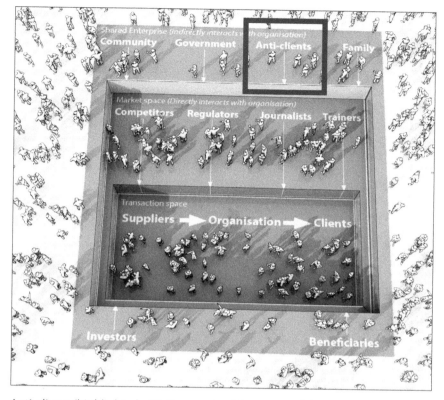

Anti-clients (highlighted with the grey box) form part of the enterprise as shown with Whole EA tool, described in chapter 3.

Most organisations still seem to prefer to ignore the complainers.
But it's perhaps not a good idea, because anticlients are the immune-system of the enterprise.
Anti-clients are metaphoric antibodies or white blood-cells of the enterprise-as-organism, protecting the integrity of the enterprise as a whole. And they can and will reject, and eject, the organisation from its place in the shared-enterprise if enough of them interpret it as a threat to the enterprise. Hence, for an organisation, monitoring the anticlient activity around itself is not merely a wise idea: it can quite literally be a matter of survival.

So how to do this?

To make sense of this, we need to understand two key points.
First, in the sense that I'm using the terms here, the enterprise is far larger than the organisation. The organisation, bounded by rules, roles and responsibilities, does its business within the scope of a shared-enterprise. An emotive idea, or story, bounded by vision, values and commitments.

Contrary to many current concepts of business, the organisation is not itself *'the enterprise',* nor does it possess the enterprise. Instead, the organisation operates *within* the enterprise. Despite its own image of itself, the organisation is unlikely to be *'the centre'* of the shared-enterprise: in reality, its existence is very much dependent on its relationships with and within the enterprise.

It's very similar to an organism's immune response: some entity within that organism *(or, here, the shared-enterprise)* is somehow identified as a threat, will become surrounded by the organism's *'guard-cells'* to shield the rest of the organism from its influence, and then either absorbed or pushed out. For a shared-enterprise, anti-clients are its antibodies, its immune system to protect itself from *'rogue'* organisations.

For an organisation, anti-client activity is the first warning-bell of an immune-response against it by the enterprise.. Just as in a living body, there'll always be some immune-system activity anyway: but alarm-bells should definitely go off as soon as that activity rises much beyond a background level. For its own survival, the organisation needs to monitor anti-client activity in the enterprise.

The scope we need to monitor here is quite a lot larger than most people seem to expect. For a start, we need to monitor within the organisation: one of the things that can definitely kill the organisation is when its own employees become anti-clients… Beyond that, we typically need to think of the *'the enterprise'* stretching out at least three steps beyond the organisation: its immediate supply-chain or value-web, its market-context, and the broader community beyond the market.

Anti-clients are people who are in the same enterprise, but disagree with how your organisation acts within that enterprise.

There are two distinct types of anti-clients for whom we need to watch: *automatic-anti-clients* and *betrayal-anti-clients*.

Automatic anti-clients are the those you will get automatically if your organisation addresses only one side of a story that includes *wicked-problems*[1]. For example, if you're building new houses, you will automatically have opposition from those who are not in favour of that particular development, as anti-clients to your organisation. By the very nature of that kind of wicked-problem, there's no way that you are not going to have someone who fiercely disagrees with you…

(At first glance, our competitors might also seem to be like anti-clients for us, but the relationship is significantly different: the opposition is peer-to-peer, not between organisation and its 'containing' broader-enterprise).

---

1. Wicked problem
An idea or problem that cannot be fixed, where there is no single solution to the problem. Wikipedia

Automatic anti-clients tend to be placed out in the outer parts of the shared-enterprise, beyond the market-space in which your organisation operates. In many cases they will reject the validity even of that market in itself, let alone any one organisation that operates within it. They are also relatively easy to identify and to monitor, because in effect *'they come with the territory'*. Their opposition is a direct outcome of a wicked-problem embedded in the core of the enterprise itself.

This does, however, also mean that there's no way to eliminate their opposition as such, because it's an outcome of the way the broader enterprise defines itself, which is far beyond our own control. The best way to tackle *automatic anti-client* risks is:

• acknowledge that the clash exists, and is automatically part of the shared-enterprise itself
• respect the opposition, and the validity of that opposition
• openly reach out to work with the anti-clients, rather than fight against them or attempt to silence or ignore them

Betrayal anti-clients are the anti-clients that your organisation creates through its actions and inactions. The *'betrayal'* in this context is a perceived betrayal by the organisation of the values or promise of the shared-enterprise, leading to a steep loss of trust in the organisation itself. Leading those to active opposition against the organisation.

Sometimes these are non-clients who don't actually engage in transactions with the organisation, but react against what they as *'uninvolved third-parties'* perceive as unfairness against others. More often, though, they are, or were, customers of the organisation who feel personally let down or betrayed by the organisation.

In that sense, *betrayal anti-clients* tend to be found more in the market-space of the enterprise, rather than in the outer areas of the shared-enterprise.

Unlike the *automatic anti-clients*, opposition from *betrayal anti-clients* often seems *'unpredictable'*, especially if the organisation is largely unaware of its impacts on others, or enacts behaviours that can seem cavalier or disrespectful about others. The opposition can also vary wildly in scope and scale, again seemingly *'without warning'*. Yet in practice these *'immune system response'* interactions are largely predictable: they arise directly from poor service-design and/or service-execution. The apparent unpredictability can also be reduced by monitoring social-media and suchlike for complaints about the organisation. A fast and respectful response is often crucial for reducing the risk that such social-media complaints could *'go viral'*.

A good way way to reduce *betrayal anti-client* risks is to do a thorough review of all services and service-relationships, looking for and then designing-out any built-in power-dysfunctions in those services.

Specifically, what we look for are two fundamental misunderstandings about power:

- **power-over**: any attempt to prop *self* up by putting *other* down
- **power-under**: any attempt to off-load responsibility onto the *other* without their engagement and consent

Unfortunately, both *power-over* and, even more, *power-under* are very common in organisations' internal and external service-relationships, in all forms and at all levels. Judging from the streams of *'online complaints, both power under and power-over are common in virtually all forms of so called 'customer-service'*; some business-models in effect depend on *power-under* or even *power-over*. This is definitely not wise, since in the days of widely-shared social-media and other forms of communication, just one disgruntled *betrayal anti-client* really can have the power to bring down an entire corporation…

In terms of actions for enterprise-architects, service-designers and others, perhaps the most crucial of all is a shift in mindset, from ignoring or rejecting *anti-client* complaints, to actively seeking them out and engaging with them. Remember that each of them is a kind of immune-response by the enterprise, against our organisation. It is the remit of the shared-enterprise, not a unilateral assertion by the organisation, that determines the continuing of our organisation's *'social-licence to operate'*.

It is tricky. On one side, every *anti-client* response represents a potential threat to that licence-to-operate; but it's likely that we, or our executives or others, won't want to hear about any complaints, will want to pretend that everything will run smoothly just how we want, without needing to face any real-world complexities or complications at all. Yet on the other side, every anti-client response provides us with information about how we could or should improve the organisation and its services. In order to better protect and expand that licence-to-operate, there's a lot that we can gain from those interactions too, if we turn round and actively engage with our anti-clients.

Anti-clients provide us with information about how we could or should improve an organisation and its services.

29: Designing for *'humans'*

In EA, how should we model a human-based 'application' such as an online customer-support service?

At first glance, this all looks really simple. As soon as we delve anywhere beneath the surface, though, it's not simple and non-trivial, and that most of the terminology we need is either non-existent or at best highly misleading.

If we don't have a clear means to describe something, it becomes very difficult to explain it to others, or engage others in creating it, or identify the problems and challenges that arise from it. Yet in this specific case, a *'human application'*, most of our existing techniques and tool-sets actively get in the way of describing what actually happens in those applications. How can we can develop usable workarounds for this problem?

Identify the problem

One of the aims of enterprise-architecture is to assist in modelling the linkages all the way from strategy to execution. A key part of this is modelling the relationships between a *'customer-view'* of a business-process, the internal execution of that process, and the technologies and infrastructures that underlie and support the process.

Some approaches focus primarily on the execution, the *'application'* itself, without much or any linkage to the customer-view and/or underlying technology.

Most enterprise-architecture frameworks describe the context-space in terms of *'layers'*. The exact numbers and labels of these layers vary from one framework to another.

In principle, these should line up well with the modelling-requirements mentioned above:

- **Business**: *'customer-view'* of a business-process
- **Application**: execution of the business-process
- **Technology**: infrastructure supporting the business-process

And in practice they do line up well, but only if the application is an automated process running on some form of computer-hardware. In many frameworks though there is no means to describe an application that is executed by people or by non-IT infrastructure, other than by crude efforts to force anything human *('manual')* into the Business layer, and anything mechanical into the Technology layer.

There also needs to be a way to describe execution of a process *('application')* that does not centre primarily or solely around the manipulation of information: relational-processes are subtly forced into the Business layer, and anything physical into the Technology layer.

In service-oriented terms, there's a very clear difference between the *'external'* provider or consumer of a service and the *'internal'* agent that enacts the service, which may be any combination of IT, human or machine.

If these points are not considered, we can end up with a mess. In practice, we can just about get away with this type of confusion if and only if our *'enterprise'*-architecture is concerned solely with IT-systems and information-based processes, and as viewed from an IT-oriented perspective.

For any other type of processes, though, or when viewed from any other perspective, such as an *'outside-in'* customer-journey, that mess can be wildly misleading, and may well render it all but impossible to describe what needs to happen within the overall architecture, or to do like-for-like comparisons of process-architectures and process-designs.

This mess will in turn make it very difficult to describe, assess or compare business-models where the viability of the business-model depends on processes that cross the relational/informational/physical boundaries. Most business-models and complete business-processes do straddle across all of those boundaries: constraining the architectural view to a single subset of the context, or randomly partitioning-off different segments of the context to separate *'architectures',* is likely to cause architectural problems or even architectural failure.

There are three key areas where these problems will be highlighted in architectural practice:

- **substitution**, themes such as business-continuity, disaster-recovery, where alternate implementations may need to be used for the same application
- **emulation**, themes where human, IT and machine capabilities are hidden behind a *'black-box'* interface that implies a different type of capability: for example, a *'manual'* capability is used with the same interface as an automated one
- **escalation**, themes where capability must be escalated across the *'Inverse-Einstein boundary'',* from rule-based or algorithmic decision-making *(which can be handled by machines or IT)* to guideline or principle-based decision-making *(which generally can't be handled by machines or IT)*

These themes will often occur in combination with each other, as we'll see in a moment, overleaf.

---

1. Inverse-Einstein boundary.
Einstein famously said that insanity is repeating the same action and expecting a different result. The opposite in the real world is that often doing the same thing can lead to different results.

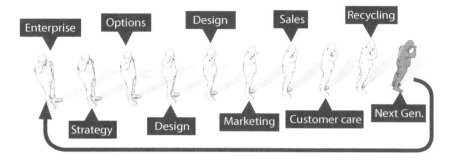

From an 'outside-in' customer-journey perspective, the ideal is that all forms of service should interweave seamlessly from one type to another.

Customer-support

Customer-support is the means by which *'external'* service-consumers can access information, advice and resolution on issues arising from the proposed, in-process or delivered service or product.

In practice, customer-support can take many forms, from self-service *(brochures, FAQs etc)* to proactive delivery of advice *(pre-sales, training and mentoring etc)* to real-time guidance *(interactive troubleshooting, help-line etc)* to off-line maintenance and repair.

From an *'outside-in'* customer-journey perspective, the ideal is that all these forms of service should interweave seamlessly from one type to another, with clear paths of action and escalation as required. The reality, however, is often far from that ideal: the various forms of customer-support service are functionally and operationally separate from each other, with the end-customer often forced to *'fill in the gaps'* for action and escalation. This is usually the result of taking an *'inside-out' (organisation-centric)* rather than *'outside-in' (customer-centric)* perspective on customer-support.

Since consistent, reliable and seamless customer-service provides distinct competitive-advantage, and is desirable in its own right for many other operational reasons, it will be useful to model not just the various forms of customer-support, but also the interrelationships between them, so as to improve the overall provision of customer-support.

Business-oriented model

This model would need to show all types of customer-support, and their substitution and escalation relationships with each other.
A service-oriented form of modelling is probably the only approach that would make consistent sense.

The core *'external'* business-role is the *customer*, in relationship to the various forms of customer support service-delivery. This should be the only role shown at the *'Business'* layer: all other human roles are at the *'Application'* layer.

In effect, each form of service-delivery is an *'application'*, in which the actual underlying method of delivery, human, IT or physical object, should be largely transparent, behind a consistent *'black-box'* type interface.

The customer seeking support should not be forced to identify which type of service-delivery best fits their needs. And especially should not be forced to exit and re-enter a different part of the overall customer-support system just to obtain a different type or escalation of advice. One of the key roles of modelling is to find ways to eliminate support-problems such as:

- FAQ with no means to escalate the query
- an array of links to different parts of the customer-*'service'* system, with no means to identify which item applies to the customer's need
- multi-layered call-option hierarchies that take far longer than a human operator to direct to the required need
- different phone-numbers for different escalation-levels or service-types, with no means to switch between them within the system
- high *'failure-demand[1]'*

The practical problem is that almost all existing business-systems, especially IT-related systems, are built on a *Taylorist[2]* model, which assumes repetitive processes delivered in linear or *'controllable'* manner by distinct specialist functions in response to predictable events.

The reality is that almost none of those criteria apply to customer-service: each enquiry is in some way unique, it rarely follows a linear path within or between *'processes'*. There is more emphasis on cross-functional generalist knowledge to link between specialists, and many of the events are by their nature unpredictable. To resolve problems with customer-support, it's therefore essential to break out of that *'linear'* mindset. And to model accordingly, to keep track of substitution and escalation, and to bring those transitions inside the organisation's overall customer service system.

1.Failure demand
When a customer has to call back the organisation to find out further information, which wastes theirs and the organisation's time.
2. Taylorist model.
Frederick Taylor in the 1880s explored using science to improve productivity in the workplace. Critics of his concepts felt that people became like cogs in machines, which might help an organisation at the expense of the workers.

⬠⬠⬠⬠⬠ *Taken from the chapter: **On human 'applications'***
in EA models

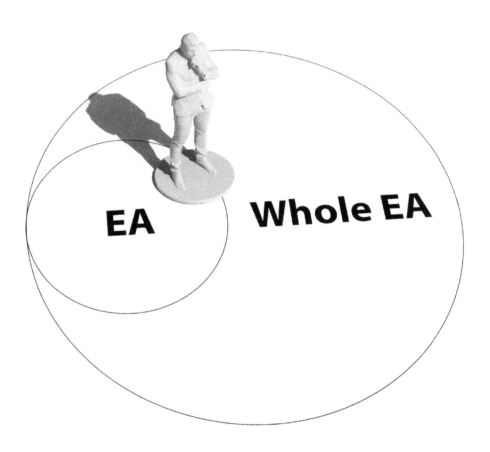

Part 4:

Whole EA perspectives

This section of the book is an abridged version of
'On Whole Enterprise Architecture'
www.leanpub.com/tp-onwholeea

30: Assumptions

When exploring how I reframe the way I work, a key part is around identifying the constraints of that work: where and how the tools work, and perhaps even more important, being clear about where they don't.

A key part of that process of framing the constraints revolves around declaring the assumptions upon which that work is based. Once we know what the assumptions are, we have a better chance of knowing where the tools are likely to work and not-work, and also what *affordances*[1] might or might not become available if and when we use the tools in unexpected ways.

The trick, of course, is in finding ways to surface those assumptions, which is not always as easy as it might seem…

Also, and important, is that this does not imply that anyone who holds different assumptions is *'wrong'*. What it does imply is that people who hold or expect or demand different assumptions than those declared here may attempt to use Whole EA in ways for which it was not designed, and so may not get the results they expect.

Here is how I best understand my own core-assumptions, and the probable implied constraints that might arise:

I assume that architecture is about how all the elements of a context work together. This includes both structure and story.

I assume that everything within a context ultimately depends on everything else. Every context or *'system'* is itself part of a larger context, and also intersects with and/or is seemingly 'composed of' any number of other sibling-contexts or sub-contexts.
Implied constraint: From that assumption, it might seem that, in order to do anything with anything, we first have to know everything about everything. We acknowledge this as an impossible ideal, yet one we should always aim for, as guided by practical limits, the classic guideline of 'Just Enough Detail'.

I assume that everywhere and nowhere is *'the Centre'* of an architecture, all at the same time, and that every service within an architecture is necessary for the viability of that architecture.

I assume that every real-world context contains inherent uncertainties, which must be explicitly acknowledged.

I assume that every alleged boundary is in part an arbitrary choice, that, for example, the boundary of a service is whatever we choose the boundary of 'the service' to be. And so that boundaries themselves should always be considered a potential subject for review within any architectural assessment.

I assume that, in enterprise-architecture, *'the enterprise'* is, in essence, an idea or intent, separate and distinct from any organisation or structure set up to act on or with that idea.

I assume that, in enterprise-architecture, the term *'the enterprise'* and its related architectures may relate to and denote any appropriate scope, rather than solely or exclusively some predefined scope. Rather than a fixed scope, I typically assume, or model in terms of, a pattern of relationships between elements in the architecture, with the relevant *'the enterprise'* extending outward beyond the element currently in architectural focus:

More generally, I also assume that the same principles of enterprise architecture can be applied at every scale, from *'really big-picture',* right down to a single web-service, and sometimes even-smaller scale than that.

I assume that architectures may be usefully described in terms of fractal-like patterns, at any scope or scale.

I assume that every real-world context contains inherent uncertainties, which must be explicitly acknowledged.

31: Competition

What's the point of competition, in a business-context? Perhaps more
to the point, what is competition in a business-context? And why?

Another of those *'obvious'* question-themes that turn out to be not so
obvious at all... And the answers are very important in EA, business-
architecture and business-model design: not least because if we get it
wrong then we'll find ourselves on a guaranteed path to business failure.

"In war, there can only be one winner". It's a popular belief, but it's wrong
in an all too literal sense. No-one wins from being involved in a war: the
only *'winners'* are those who take care not to be involved, and the parasites
who profit from picking up the pieces afterwards. We'll see why that's so in a
moment, and also why that fact matters a very great deal in business.

So is competition good, or not good? For that matter, should we cooperate
with others, or not? In all of those questions, the obvious answer is
"It all depends...". But what it most depends on in each case is what we
understand as **the nature and purpose of competition**, and its apparent
counterpart in cooperation. And that, in turn, depends on what we
understand as **the nature and purpose of power**.

What's the purpose of competition? Is it to win? If so, win what?

Is it to beat the other guy? If so, what happens next?

Or is it less about winning as such, but more about not having to face the
feeling of failure, of being labelled *'the loser'*, and everything else that goes
with that label in so many societies?

Behind most of the myths of competition is a hugely tangled mess of
mostly-unacknowledged feelings and fears. The details change from culture
to culture, but the real core of it is a really simple set of mistakes about the
nature of power in the workplace and elsewhere. In essence what it comes
down to is this:

The physics definition is that **power is the ability to do work**.

Most social definitions are closer to the notion that **power is the
ability to avoid work**.

Therein lie the roots of some serious problems for business...

In the myths around *'winning'* and *'losing'*, most of the work being avoided
is relational and aspirational: in other words, work that can only be personal,
not collective. On one side, it's often a failure to grasp that, on a finite
world, we are always in a closed, finite context where ultimately there is no

convenient-scapegoat *'them'*, but only *'us'*, so there is no-one that we can *'win'* against. On the other side, we actually can't force others to face our own feelings for us, no matter how much we would want that to happen, because they're actually our feelings. And in reality there's no way to win, in any real sense, unless we find the courage to turn round and face that work. Rather than wasting what little energy we have in futilely trying and, by definition, failing to *'export'* it to everyone else.

Do we really think we can *'win'* by making someone else 'lose'? The reality is that the most we could achieve is a temporary respite from that *'feeling-work'*, at the cost of actually increasing the damage and the load across the overall system. At best, we gain a short-lived *'high'*, exactly like any other form of addiction. Which is why most of the myths about *'winning'*, and most of the myths about *'beating the competition'*, are a literally deadly delusion.

Competition is good: we need competition if we're to improve our skills, our competencies, our overall game.

But it's only good, is only successful, in the longer term, if we compete *with* others. Not *'against'* others.

Cooperation is good: we need cooperation if we're to do anything that we cannot do solely on our own.

But although cooperation is always going to mean working with others in some sense or other, it's only good, is only successful, in the longer term, if the overall aim of the cooperation is *with* all others. Not *'against'* others.

There are only two choices here: either everyone wins, in some way; or everyone loses. There is no *'win/lose'*: it's a form of *'lose/lose'*, in which an apparent gain for one party masks a greater overall loss for everyone, including the *'winner'*.

If we compete with others, and with ourselves, everyone wins. Sometimes one player is *'the winner'*, sometimes another: but overall, over time, everyone wins in one sense or another, and the overall *'competing'* is a key part of what helps everyone win.

If we compete against others... well, in short, everyone loses. No matter what it looks like in the shorter-term, everyone loses.
And there's no way round any of that: all of that comes from the real nature of power itself.

So if we're going to compete, and in business, we're going to want to compete, and also often have to compete, then we have to compete with others, not against them. Because if we don't, we're going lose, even, or perhaps most, when we seem most to *'win'*.
Which is no doubt somewhat different from what we'd hear in most

everyday ideas about *'business as usual'.* But it's also the only way that works. Which can be difficult, especially in enterprise architectures and the like, where we do need to deliver something that actually does work.

Implications in business-architecture and EA

In architectural terms, what all of this comes down to is one very simple fact:

• every instance of *'competition-against',* in any form whatsoever, represents an active source for loss of overall effectiveness, and a potential point for catastrophic-collapse of the overall architecture

That applies right up to an overall business-model, onward through design of performance-bonuses of sales, or managers' resource allocation, right down to real-time relationships between web-services and code-level conflicts. Competition-with is *(usually)* good: no doubt about that. Yet every time we allow some form of competition-against to slip through and become embedded in the system-structures, we increase the risk of total system-failure.

Which leads us to one very simple test:

• *wherever the architecture includes some form of competition, is it competition-with, or competition-against?*

In many cases, perhaps most, we'll want our architecture to encourage competition-with.

Yet we must eliminate every form of competition-against, otherwise we're designing an architecture that, by definition, is designed to fail.

Architecturally, the only thing that makes it hard is artificial boundaries between segments of the overall system. This is one area where we need a whole-of-system perspective. For much the same reasons, we need people to see that the overall enterprise runs on a great deal more than just money. This is possible: more to the point, it's all been done, and proven in practice, too. And overall it's quite easy to prove that competition with is more efficient and effective than competition-against.

There is, however, one serious structural problem of which we need to become very much aware. Competition-with is the only way that works, but sadly a lot of organisations still believe that they can be *'the winner'* in any game of competition-against.

Yet unfortunately the game is naturally weighted in a way that props up those delusions. We know that win/win is the only way that works; we know that we can only win if others win too. But if they believe in win/lose, then they'll be certain that they can only win by *'making'* others seem to lose.

In other words, whenever we come across someone like that, we want them to win, but they want us to lose, which is not a good place for us to be…
In those circumstances, to quote the old film *War Games*, *"the only way to win is to not play"*. So once we do get properly onto competition-with, we cannot engage with anyone who indulges in competition-against, because we will always lose, in one sense or another, whenever that occurs.

In fact everyone will lose whenever that occurs, but it's our organisation for which we're designing the architecture, so that's what needs to be our focus here.

So that test, explicitly excluding any interaction with any form of competition-against, needs to be embedded right the way through every aspect of the architecture, without exception.

With some people , *"the only way to win is to not play"*.

32: Digital transformation check-lists

Digital-transformation is most likely to succeed when it's based on principles of service-design and service-management. The following transformation-checklist can be applied to all forms and modes of service-delivery, not just IT-based, but any appropriate combinations of people, machines and IT.

1. Service strategy
Do we have clarity on how concepts of service will apply throughout organisational strategy?

Many of these themes will be familiar to service managers. Note, though, that this can often extend far beyond IT, in that everything in the enterprise either is, represents or implies a service. We also need to explore the linkages between strategy, tactics, operations, change learning and more, as per the generic governance-model described earlier.

2. Service design
Do we have clarity on how to design and redesign services that match the organisation's changing needs?

Some of the key themes for this, such as service-catalogues, service availability, service-levels and suchlike, will be familiar to service managers through standards. Again, though, this applies not just to IT-based services, but to all types of services, and the interactions between them. It also applies to handovers and substitutions between service-types, such as in switching over to an equivalent manual process during disaster-recovery. Note also that this applies to design for how smaller-scope services can be grouped into larger-scope services, and for dynamically-constructed services and processes specific to each customer's needs.

3. Service transition
Do we have clarity on *how to change our services,* to match the organisation's changing needs, without disrupting service operations?

The key themes for this will be familiar to service managers, though these will, again, usually need to be extended to cover a scope much broader than IT alone. One further theme to consider here is how service-transition intersects with service-operations, such as where software-updates may be deployed automatically many times per day, or where services are changed on-the-fly for specific customers or for A/B-testing and the like.

4. Service operation
Do we have clarity on how our services are operating, in terms of delivering to enterprise needs?
(continued overleaf)

The key themes for this can be found in service-management standards, with concerns such as reliability, efficiency, incident-capture and so on, but also about capture of insights and ideas for improvement that arise from within the process of operations itself. Once again, this must also apply to all types of service-delivery and service-operations, not solely to IT-services.

5. Continual service improvement
Do we have clarity on how to support continual improvement of services?

This builds on themes that should be familiar to most service managers. The key concern here is to ensure that these principles are actively applied in real-world practice, not just talked about as a good idea.

6. Service value-management
Do we have clarity on how to ensure that services keep on-track to enterprise values?

For service managers, some aspects of this would be addressed via standards, but often there'll also be much more. For example, whilst this would include IT-related aspects of security management, financial management and suchlike, an organisation will also need to cover enterprise-wide value-concerns such as health and safety, financial-probity, and many others. For each of these enterprise-values, you'll need distinct support services that explain why that value is important in the enterprise: provide training and skills-development in how to support that value within every action; provide run-time tracking of factors relevant to that value; and guide continuous-learning from the outcomes of every action. The respective set of enterprise-values would be derived from the enterprise-story: identifying these is a key first step in any business-transformation.

7. Service management for transformation
Finally, do we have clarity on how to address the complexities of business-transformation?

For service managers, this draws some of its themes from standards, but extends to address the far greater complexities of digital-transformation. One example here relates to the classic quality-concern of *'garbage in, garbage out'*: both big-data and machine-learning can actually be dangerous if the data they rely on is of questionable quality. The success of that business-transformation would thus depend not just on the respective technologies, but also the quality-assurance services for all of the data-sources that feed into those systems.

*Taken from the chapter: **A services-checklist for digital-transformation***

33: Which EA tools to use?

The most important EA tools are pen and paper, or whiteboard and sticky-notes.

Less visibly, ***the real tool there is conversation***, as a means to get all parties to think and re-think about what they are all doing, what they want to do, why they are doing it, and how to get from here to there.

In a social context ***the space is often an important tool***, too: it often makes a lot of difference as to whether it's in a meeting,room, someone's office, a cafe or a bar.

Of course there are many software based EA tools. The core advantage of all of the computer-based tools is that they deliver clean, professional-looking diagrams. The purpose built *'EA tools'* also do this in accordance with defined modelling rules, link everything together in consistent ways, and provide a consistent, known place to store everything. The more expensive tools justify their sometimes very high price-tags by the quality of their collaboration-features and of the information-repository beneath the surface, making them appropriate for shared use across large organisations.

Disadvantages too, though. The simpler graphic tools don't really support consistency or structure: it's just a diagram, with nothing much behind it. The so-called *'EA-tools'* often aren't much about EA at all, but more about solution-architecture and system-design. Those are activities that happen after EA, or around EA, but not the real core of EA itself. And some of those tools, need to be improved to make them more usable, more resilient and more tolerant of user-error.

The other real danger of computer-based tools is that they can trick us into thinking that the real product of EA is a bunch of diagrams. Those diagrams are useful, and often important for communication. But they're just the *'how'* and *'with-what'* of EA; what we need to keep the focus on, much more, is the *'why'* of the architecture.
The real product of EA is not the diagrams, but the social process by which we arrived at those diagrams, which is not the same thing at all.
And unfortunately it seems that the better the *'EA tool'* is at managing the diagrams and the repositories behind them, the worse it seems to be at supporting the messy, always-uncertain thinking-process that is at the core of EA.
Getting the balance right is not easy, and each type of tool does it in a different way, which is why most of us end up abandoning the search for *'the perfect EA tool'*, and accept the mess of working with a mass of individually useful yet often incompatible tools.

**Over the years I have developed various tools, some of which are
mentioned in this book.**
Some others are featured in the *Tools for Change-mapping* book:

The Sense-making Tool
Before trying to resolve an issue you need to know what the issue is, why
does it happen and so on. Once you know this you will be better placed to
resolve it.

The Visioning Tool
This version of the tool is used by an organisation to define what is the
issue that affects an enterprise, what is done to address it and why it
needs addressing. This will act as an anchor to check against all *their*
strategic decisions.

Enterprise Canvas
This version of the tool is used as a visual checklist to understand what a
service does, why it does it and what an organisation needs to effectively
run that service.

The Guide Tool
This version of the tool helps an organisation define what must stay
constant and what can change when resolving an issue.

The Service Cycle Tool
This tool looks at each stage of the customer journey from the view of the
your customer and your organisation.

The Effectiveness Tool
This tool acts as guidance across the organisation and is referred to when
resolving issues or as part of the enterprise.

The SEMPER Tool
This version of SEMPER is used to measure staff member's ability to do work
within an organisation. Rather than arbitrarily assigning blame, a more
accurate picture can show what is actually happening.

The SCORE Tool
This version of the tool is used to explore what capabilities an organisation
has or lacks to resolve an issue. This version of the tool follows a similar basic
logic to **SWOT** *(designed by Albert Humphrey).*

The SCAN Tool
This version of the tool is used before resolving an issue, to find out what is
known and what isn't when resolving that issue.

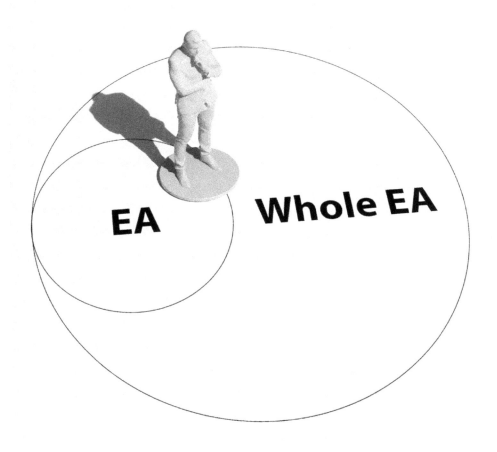

EA

Whole EA

Part 5:

How not to fail in EA

This section of the book is a small part of
'How not to fail in enterprise architecture'
www.leanpub.com/tp-notfail

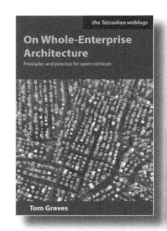

the Tetradian weblogs

On Whole-Enterprise Architecture
Principles and practice for open contexts

Tom Graves

34: Beware of *'policy-based evidence'*

Sometimes politicians declare *'success'* over a project, on the basis of noticeably-selective short-term *'evidence'.' Success'* that in the longer term, when faced with more rigorous assessment, turned out to be of limited value at best, or, too many cases, expensively worse-than-useless.

Part of this is an outcome of *Gooch's Paradox*, that *'things not only have to be seen to be believed, but also have to be believed to be seen'.* In this case, only that which is believed becomes that which is seen. *'Evidence'*, in its most literal sense of the term, with all counter-evidence ignored or dismissed from view precisely because the possibility of its existence is not believed.

It arises from any of a whole suite of cognitive-errors, ranging from excessive-zeal to scientific-incompetence, and worse. We need to be aware to expect it wherever there is some form of vested-interest, whether personal, social, commercial or whatever. For example, the all-too common dangers implied in the old warning of *"never expect someone to 'get it' if their income, job or status depends on not getting it"*.

The real danger is that *'policy-based evidence'* is frequently used to support policies based on circular-reasoning. In business, the more obvious examples include IT-centrism and managerialism. Respectively, that *'the answer'* to any business problem is more IT, or more managers and more managerial *'control'. (The two are often blended together, of course, with IT providing the supposed means for 'control'.)*

For viable policy and system-design, it's essential to think in terms of whole systems, not isolated linear-causalities. Otherwise we will exacerbate or even create *'wicked-problems'.* Instead, in circular-policy, policy based on circular-reasoning and *'policy-based evidence'*, a random subset of a whole system is selected as *'the problem'.* And, very often, a single element interacting with or within that subset is randomly selected as *'the cause'.* Attention is paid only to the impact of that *'the cause'* on that *'the problem'*: this may be either positive *('the cause is the only answer to the problem')* or negative *('the cause is exclusively to blame for the problem')*.
From the outside, and from this specific perspective, it all seems to *'make sense',* and fits well with the kind of linear, non-ambiguous, non-systemic models of causality that so many people still seem to prefer. Whether or not they can actually be relied upon in any real-world context. Yet because attention is paid only to that one *'cause',* what we get from it is *'policy-based evidence'*, that self-selected subset of the whole.
And since the *'evidence'* supports the assumptions of the policy, because it is selected to fit the assumptions of the policy, this is then taken as justification and *'proof'* that the policy itself is correct. In other words, a perfect self-confirming circularity, explicitly excluding any means to test against a broader reality.

Implications for enterprise-architecture

Enterprises and organisations of all kinds are riddled with *'policy-based evidence'*. The problem, is that, especially if left unchecked, every instance of *'policy-based evidence'* has potential to cause serious damage to the overall enterprise. It is not something that we can safely ignore.

First, we need to be able to identify *'policy-based evidence.'* What makes this hard, and potentially problematic in a business-politics sense, is that so much of it can seem *'normal',* and/or that highlighting any example at all from that flood of information may itself be misinterpreted as some form of bias or prejudice on our part. To make a start, though, look for some of the more obvious clues, where:

• attention is continually dragged back to a single *'the cause'* or *'the solution'*
• there is explicit rejection *(or even active silencing)* of counter-evidence or counter-examples, *"that's only a special-case, it never happens"*, *"the exception proves the rule"*, and so on
• there are hints and more of *'follow the money',* the interests of a self-selected individual or sub-group have been arbitrarily prioritised over the aims and balances of the enterprise as a whole

Having identified a potential example, model the respective context as a mutually-interactive, mutually-interdependent system, so as to highlight hidden assumptions that underpin the *'evidence.'* However, it's crucially important to:

• model the system in an open and transparent manner, highlighting all assumptions made in the modelling process, to counter any accusation of bias or prejudice on our own part
• counter and resist all attempts to force the modelling back into a subset linear-causality frame. In some cases the pressures to give in on this point may be intense, but surrendering to a linear-causality-only view of a systemic context will allow the hidden assumptions behind the *'policy based evidence'* to be re-concealed, and will defeat the entire object of the modelling exercise

This kind of exploration can be fraught with all manner of political dangers: there are a lot of vested-interests behind any form of *'policy-based evidence'*, and those *'interested-parties'* may well react, sometimes to the extreme, if their pseudo-evidence is questioned. Done carelessly, or done wrong, this can be a real career-killer, or worse: for each one of us, from a personal perspective, it's probably one of the most difficult and dangerous parts of enterprise-architecture work that there is.

The catch is that this work must be done, if the enterprise and its architectures are to succeed, be effective, on-purpose. This is a fact which puts us, as enterprise-architects, on an often-unintended, yet necessary, direct collision-course with a lot of people.

One definition of *'stakeholder'* is *'anyone who can wield a sharp stake in our direction'*: we're likely to discover here just how accurate that joke really is...

In practice, often the only thing that can make this in any way safe *(or safer, at any rate)* is to be fully open and transparent in all of the assessment, and in all of the reasoning that goes into it. This is because doing so leaves aggressive stakeholders where an attack on the reasoning would itself expose their own unfounded prejudices.

Note too that the challenges, and the tactics we need to employ, are essentially the same regardless of the source of *'policy-based evidence'* and the resulting architectural-challenges that we need to resolve.
The analysis, assessment, modelling and identification of *'missing factors'* are all straightforward enough, for any competent enterprise-architect: it's only the politics of it, and the emotional loading behind all of that, that make it all so fraught.

Policy-based evidence

We need to be able to identify 'policy-based evidence'. But so much of it can seem 'normal', inside a flood of information.

⬠⬠⬠⬠⬠ *Taken from the chapter:* **Beware of *'policy-based evidence'***

35: Certification

Each autumn, up would come the new crop of graduates, each with their
shiny new graduation-certificate and their own absolute certainty that they
knew absolutely everything that there was to know about engineering.
It was the job of the workshop-foreman to show them that they didn't…

There was a *'work-to-rule'*: the fitters and turners in the workshop were told
to make exactly what the new graduates specified in their engineering-
drawings, even if it didn't make sense. Which meant that the technicians
turned out parts that wouldn't fit, or that couldn't be assembled, or would
corrode or collapse in minutes even if they could be assembled.

The graduates, of course, would shout and scream that the technicians had
done it all wrong, that they hadn't properly followed the design. At which
point the workshop-foreman and, usually, a senior-engineer or two, would
take each graduate gently through their drawings and show them what
actually has to happen in the real world, where perfect-in-theory rarely
matches up to the confusions of the real world. And where a quite
different kind of knowledge, the practical knowledge that the technicians
had honed over so many years at the workbench, would also need to be
brought to bear if the designs were ever actually to work.

Which, by a roundabout route, brings us to a really important
topic in EA: ***the over-certainties of certification***.

As with most technical fields, enterprise-architecture is becoming riddled
with all manner of 'certification'-schemes

Certification-schemes do have their place, and a useful role to play, in
some cases and some circumstances. But if misused, all that a so-called
'certification' actually certifies may be that someone has just enough
knowledge to really get into trouble on any real-world project, but with not
enough knowledge to get out of it.

Something we can do is to get a bit more clarity about what we mean when
we say that *"certification-schemes do have their place"*.

What is their place, exactly? In what ways and in what contexts is
certification useful, or, perhaps more important, not-useful?
What can we use to tell the difference between them?

For example, a first-level trainee isn't likely to be much use without
some basic training, usually at least a day's-worth, in most real-world
contexts. And they're not likely to develop much beyond a certain point
without some solid idea of the theory that applies in that context, enough to
communicate meaningfully with others who do know more than they do.

To go further, that apprentice needs to gain a better grasp of the ambiguities and uncertainties of the trade, as a working *'journeyman'.* And in almost any real discipline, it will take a long time, typically at least five years or so, or 10,000 hours, of study and real-world practice.

There is another progression going on here: from practice to theory. The theory of certainty, and then from the theory of uncertainty, or complexity, back towards a very different kind of real-world practice.

That, at least, is the traditional skills-development model, always grounded in real-world practice. Yet the old class-hierarchies, carried through into present-day business-practices, assert a strict separation of roles: *'higher-class'* officers and managers need learn only the theory, and sit back and tell *'the workers'* what to do. While *'low-class'* labourers are deemed incapable of thought, and must do all of the dirty real-world work, without ever being allowed to question or to answer back.
Which is not only arrogant but really ineffective in practice, and long since been proven to be as well. But unfortunately it's still a very popular idea. The result is that we end up with a whole class of people who've learnt all of the theory, yet with little to no real grasp of the real-world practice.

One of the most dangerous delusions that this model teaches is the idea that everything can be reduced to *'rational'* control. When we combine this with the theory-centric view of the world, where doing practical work is always *Somebody Else's Problem.* And in which that *'Somebody Else'* can always be derided or blamed if the assumptions of theory don't work in practice, then we can end up with people who have a distorted view of the context.

We can derive a distinct description of what each type of certification-study should cover, and exactly what the respective certification-exam should test:

Trainee skill-level:
• study: work-instructions; application of work-instructions in live practice; how to identify when to escalate to someone with greater experience
• test: ability to deliver specified results within acceptable tolerances; ability to identify when not to do the work *(to not transition from non-competence to incompetence)*

Apprentice skill-level:
• study: shared-terminology; theory behind work-instructions *(various levels of theory)*; links between theory and practice; reasoning from the particular to the general
• test: knowledge of theory as per specified *'laws'* and so on; ability to derive particular cases within the specified constraints of those *'laws'*

Journeyman skill-level:
- study: complexity, ambiguity, uncertainty, probability, possibility; adaptation from the general to the particular *(context-specific)*
- test: knowledge of theory of uncertainty, and theory underpinning guidelines for working with uncertainty; ability to identify when a context is outside of expected constraints, and how to ascertain the actual constraints *(and probable dynamics of constraints)* applying in a given context

Master skill-level:
- study: practical application in partly or fully-unique contexts, in multiple and often interleaving *(repeating)* time-scales
- test: ability to respond appropriately to unique and/or unpredicted or unpredictable circumstances, often in real-time; ability to innovate and contribute personally to the development of the discipline

In practice, it's all but impossible to assess and validate *'master'*, level skills through any conventional kind of repeatable *'test',* because they're about dealing with the unique or unrepeatable. The usual test-method there is via peer-review, and even that can be problematic if the person's work is unique enough to have no direct peers. A very long way from the over-certainties of certifications, anyway…

There's one additional very important point here, around the use of automated-testing with preset-answers, such as in a multiple-choice exam: a certification based on match against preset answers is not valid as a test of competence for any skill-level that needs to work in contexts of uncertainty. Multiple-choice tests should not be used for anything that involves any significant degree of unorder in a context. For example:

- a multiple-choice exam is a good means to test for knowledge and correct usage of terminology *(a typical focus for a 'Foundation'-level exam)*
- a multiple-choice exam is not a good means to test for knowledge for how to adapt best-practices to a given context *(a typical requirement for a 'Practitioner'-level exam)*

Some of the *'certifications'* in the enterprise-architecture space at present seem to be based on automated multiple-choice exam, and do not provide any means to test for linkage between theory and practice. Although this is acceptable for basic *'Foundation'* level skills, it is problematic for skills of any higher level. The theory-only focus and random *'truth'* assertions will test only for ability to pass the test, not for competence in real-world practice. Worse, such tests are unable to distinguish between lack of knowledge, versus higher competence in dealing with uncertainty. Both groups are likely to give answers that are *'wrong'* according to the test's own limited constraints and so tend to award highest test-scores to those who are not able to deal with real-world ambiguity. That is a test-outcome that can be highly misleading, and even dangerous, to anyone who relies on the

certification-scheme as an actual metric of competence.
What's also interesting here is that humility and self-honesty tends
to follow the same curve:

- trainees know that they don't know *(much)*
- apprentices know that they know more than trainees, and that what they
  know is *'the truth'*
- journeyman-level practitioners are always in the process of relearning the
  discomforts of ambiguity and uncertainty, where *'truth'* tends often to be
  somewhat relative
- masters can usually be identified by their willingness to accept that the
  more they know, the less they really know

Which, overall, leaves us with the unfortunate tendency that those who
know the most theory and the least of the practice are also those who are
most certain of themselves and their knowledge. And, often, the most vocal
in asserting their certainty of knowledge, yet in reality will often have the
least applicable or useful knowledge. A rather importance distinction…

A trainee learns the instructions, an apprentice learns the theory,
a journeyman learns that theory doesn't always fit practice and a master
accepts the more they know, the less they know.

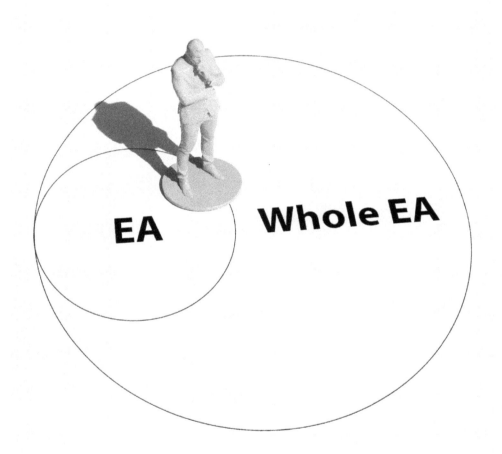

EA   Whole EA

Part 6:

Appendix

This section of the book suggests a simple
checklist for running projects and further reading.

36: A simple checklist

In this section of the book is a simple checklist which can be used when attempting to resolve an issue.

The A-B tool

This tool *(shown overleaf)* aims to break down most of the stages of a project. It is split into two main phases. The first *(A)* goes from when an issue is raised to when it resolved. The second *(B)* covers what happens **after**. Often what happens after an issue has been resolved actually determines how effective that resolution was. For example *'clean-up'* after producing something can be more costly than producing an item, such as to the natural environment.

The idea of the tool is to look at these stages **before** they happen, as this may influence the design of the project, before it is resolved. It is far easier to amend a pencil sketch than a *'in-production'* product, for example.

These questions are not meant to be exhaustive, rather to start discussions.

Let us imagine the issue we want to resolve is whether to to upgrade an airport's security screening system and ask these *types* of questions:

Phase A

Context:
Set the project in context of the enterprise, why are you trying to solve the issue? Should it be resolved or left as it is? Who are the stakeholders inside the enterprise? What are the vision and values of the enterprise? How does the enterprise benefit if it is solved? How does politics, economics, social factors and technology from outside your organisation factor? Where does your organisation fit inside the enterprise?

Strategy:
Does resolving the issue fit into your organisation's overall strategy?
Are you attempting to resolve the issue because you choose to, or are external factors forcing you to resolve the issue? Is this project out of scope from what you normally do? Do you have the right people in place to resolve the issue?

Market research:
Is there a demand for the issue to be resolved? Is somebody solving it already? Are you improving your existing offer, or are you offering a brand new solution? Does the technology exist to allow you to resolve your issue?

Management/Support:
Do you have people who will fight for the project and keep it and everyone else on track? Do they actually know how to manage a project like this?

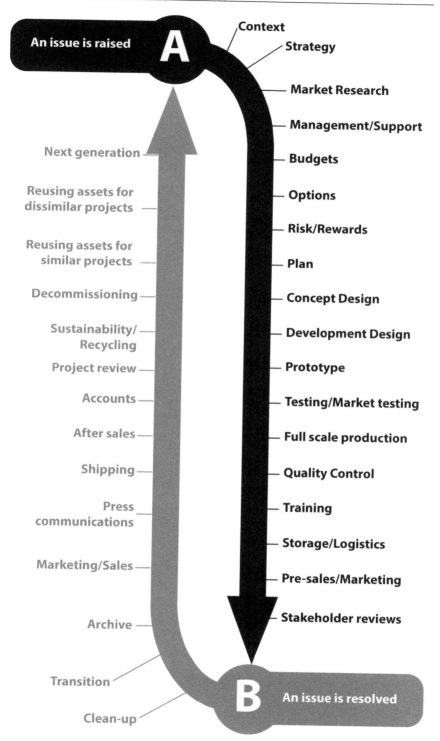

An issue is raised

A

Context
Strategy
Market Research
Management/Support
Budgets
Options
Risk/Rewards
Plan
Concept Design
Development Design
Prototype
Testing/Market testing
Full scale production
Quality Control
Training
Storage/Logistics
Pre-sales/Marketing
Stakeholder reviews

Next generation
Reusing assets for dissimilar projects
Reusing assets for similar projects
Decommissioning
Sustainability/ Recycling
Project review
Accounts
After sales
Shipping
Press communications
Marketing/Sales
Archive
Transition
Clean-up

B An issue is resolved

Any project can be split into two distinct phases

Budget:
Do you have a realistic budget in terms of finances, time, people, skills, equipment, locations to actually resolve the issue?

Options
What are your options for resolving the issue? Are there more effective methods you wouldn't normally consider?

Risks/Rewards:
What happens if things go horribly wrong? What are unlikely but possible outcomes? What are some unexpected positives that might arise?

Plan
Have you jumped to planning without fully understanding why you want to resolve the issue? Is the plan realistic? Have you tested the plan in real world conditions?

Concept Design:
Are you exploring multiple ways to resolve the issue? For example thumbnail sketches produced quickly to explore multiple approaches, not just the first one which comes to you.

Development Design:
Are you considering the fine details which can bring a whole project grinding to a halt? What are the dependencies? What needs to be done before other things can continue? Are you considering the user, how will someone actually use something you design to resolve your issue?

Prototype
Do you have a working prototype ready to face real world issues outside the comfort of a computer, such as dust, confused users?

Testing/Market testing:
Are you testing you solution in *'ideal'* conditions or more realistic conditions? Have you tested it in brutal conditions? Do you need to strengthen your design for these possible conditions? In regards to the market, what do people think? Do you need to tune your design?

Full scale production:
How will you actually produce production versions? Do you have the infrastructure to do that? Do you have the resources in place?

Quality control:
Are there bugs and errors which make the resolution ineffective? Will the resolution stay resolved, or is it a quick fix, that will need even further repairs later on?

Training:
Will people need training in order to take advantage of your issue being resolved, or is it so complicated that people will just use something else?

Storage/Logistics:
Once you have resolved your issue, will it need storing somewhere, who will be able to access it? Once you have resolved your issue, how will you actually get it to those that need it?

Pre-sales/marketing
Are new customers/users aware of what you are trying to achieve? Does there seem to be a positive response, if not why?

Stakeholder review
Are all stakeholders receptive to your proposed resolution? Is it actually solving what it was meant to?

By this stage we can visualise (with more detailed questions asked) if resolving the issue would bring benefit to all. Again the idea of the tool is to look into the future, before doing anything.

The next phase now imagines the issue has been resolved and what happens *after*, as what we find here may influence our design. In a way looking as if we had already resolved the issue and looking back.

Phase B

Clean-up
If we imagine your issue has been resolved successfully, but at what cost? Does the resolving of the issue need such a clean-up that it might have been better not to have bothered in the first place?

Transition
Will people need time to transition from the old resolution to the new? What happens in the meantime, will things just stop while the issue is resolved? Or will the resolution have to happen while the current solution exists?

Archive
With all the effort you took to resolve the issue, did you record how you did it? What happens if the team that resolved the issue, leave? What happens if somebody has to undo what you did, years later?

Marketing/sales
If the resolution is a product or service, how will people know it exists? How will they obtain it? How much would it cost for them to purchase it? Do they understand the benefits your resolution (*should*) bring to them? And do you?

Press communications
Does anyone even know what you did to resolve the issue? Are there stakeholders that should be made aware, in case they are impacted?

Shipping
How will you get the resolution to those that need it? Are you reliant on other parties, that might not be as concerned as you are?

After-sales
How do people get help using your resolution? Are there actual people to help? Is your resolution turning clients into anti-clients? What happens if your resolution breaks?

Accounts
Was your resolution financially successful? Did it use so many resources that its benefits are negated?

Project review
Did you do what you set out to do? What went wrong? What went right? Was the plan effective in real world conditions?
What would you do differently?

Sustainability/recycling
Is your resolution using resources effectively and considerately? How much waste was generated? Once your resolution reaches the end of its life, is it going to be possible to recycle? How would it be recycled and by who?

Decommissioning
Eventually your resolution will need replacing. How would you do that? Is it going to be so costly or even dangerous to replace in the future, it might be better to approach *this* resolution differently? When would it be decommissioned and by who? Why might it be decommissioned?

Reusing assets for similar projects
Now that you have spent all this time producing a resolution, could it be used for similar projects?

Reusing assets for dissimilar projects
Could the assets created in this resolution have unexpected uses in different contexts?

Next-generation
While the obvious focus might be on resolving your issue now, eventually it will likely need replacing, possibly with a next-generation version. What might that look like? Considering how easy it would it be transition from this generation to the next? What features could be in there, and why are they not in there now? When do think a next-generation version would be needed?

Back to Phase A

Looking at how your brand-new solution itself will one day need replacing, may influence how you design your solution. One of the key approaches might be *'design for disassembly'*. Considering what your shiny new idea might look like in 10 years from now, or 30 years from now. Wonder-solutions many years later can be extremely difficult to dismantle.

So with this tool we can, in a way, travel into the future and look back at what we do differently, **before** we actually change anything.

37: What's next?

This book is made up of a few curated articles from the large Tetradian anthologies which go into more depth, these can be found at **www.leanpub.com/u/tetradian**

This book is also supported by the *Change-mapping* series, which is a step by step method, based on the **Five Elements** method. The three books describe how to explore and resolve any issue, of any size and complexity.

The Change-mapping series of books based on the Five Elements method.

The first book describes the basics, such as how to set up a *Change-mapping* mission to explore an issue. The second book introduces a set of tools to help add more detail to your missions, while the last book includes a complete step by step of a detailed mission.

"Change-mapping' deserves to be part of the start-up kit of every cross-functional team that is about to tackle a complex business challenge - be it a business model adjustment, organisational change or operational problem."
Daniel Poso, PhD - Global Head, Digital Transformation Strategy, Product Development, Roche AG

"I warmly recommend this book to change agents who are searching for a pragmatic change method and tools that make their impact felt immediately. I am sure you will find the tools and ideas presented valuable and gracefully challenging conventional practices. I wish I had known some of these tools much sooner in my career.."
Jörg Schreiner, Managing partner Co-shift

Each book is around 125 pages and is out now on Amazon.